EAST HARLEM
The Postwar Years
LEO GOLDSTEIN

EAST HARLEM
The Postwar Years
LEO GOLDSTEIN

Preface by **JUAN GONZÁLEZ**

Introduction by **A. D. COLEMAN**

powerHouse Books

Brooklyn, NY

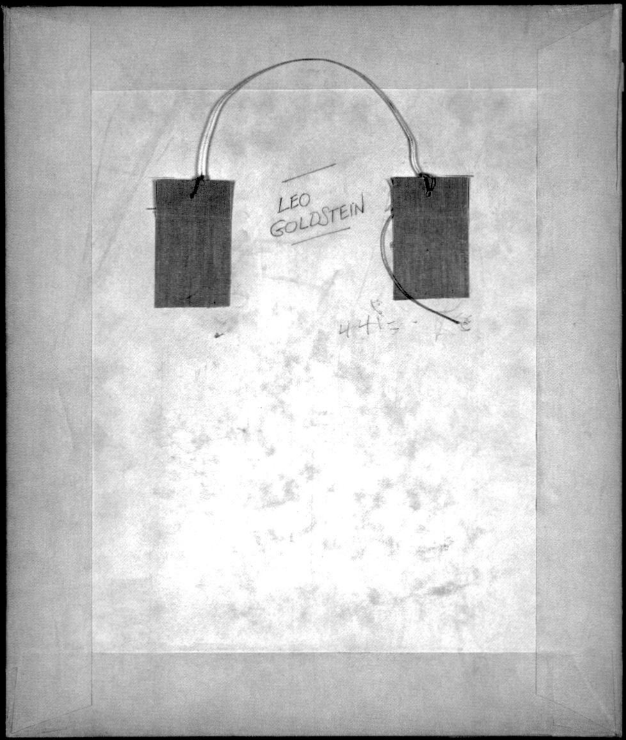
LEO
GOLDSTEIN

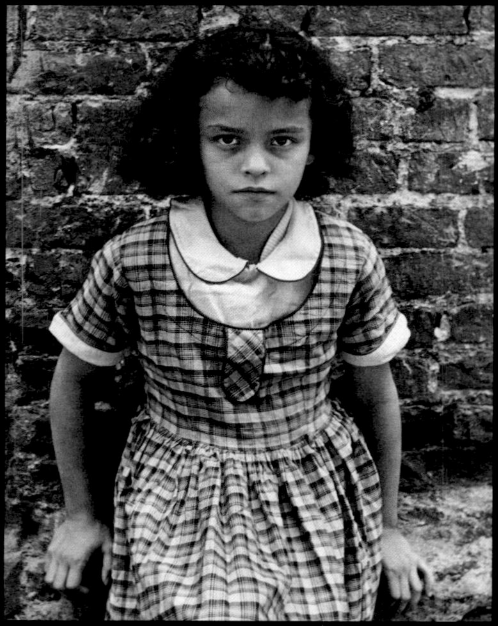

Edited by Régina Monfort
and produced in collaboration with
Naomi Goldstein

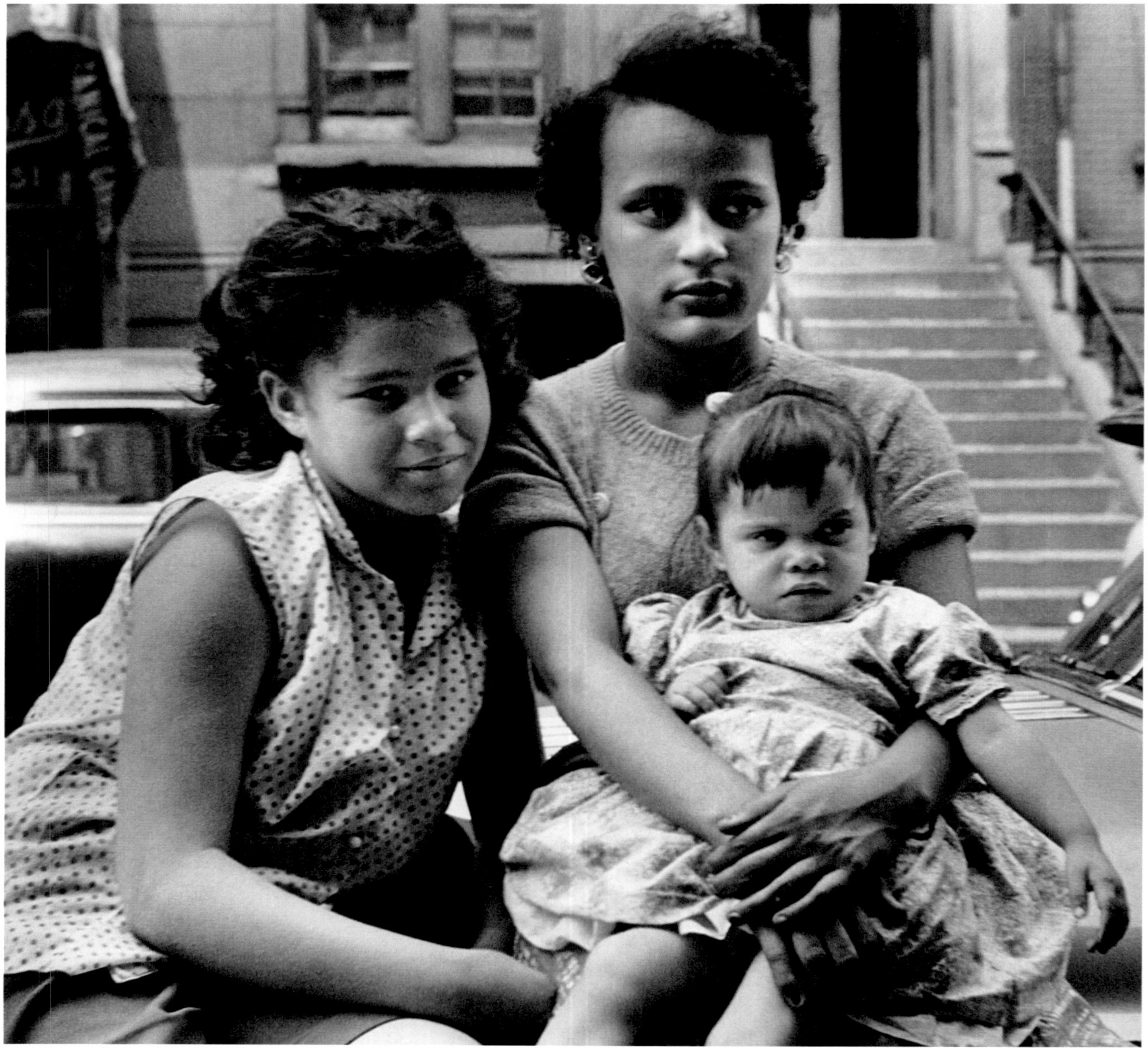

 Mother and daughters, c.1950

Preface by Juan González

City sidewalks teem with brown-skinned children at play while their grandmothers keep a watchful eye over them from a nearby window. Whole families return home from a shopping trip to *La Marqueta*. Storefront bodegas and tenement stoops are filled with teenagers and adults who congregate by day or night for some respite from the stifling summer heat. They gather after a long day of work just to socialize with neighbors (this was long before television, cable, and internet), or to enjoy the familiar rhythmic melodies of their homeland wafting from a corner music store. A startling array of young and old gaze out at the camera with haunting eyes that radiate both wonder and fear, both wariness and warmth, both the hope and the pain of migrants from a faraway countryside as they strive to make sense of a strange new world of asphalt streets and dreary concrete buildings.

This was the East Harlem neighborhood where I grew up during the 1950s, the same world Leo Goldstein captured so perfectly in splendid photos of both its inhabitants and its stark terrain, whether shoeshine boys on a street corner or a cuchifrito vendor at work, whether a lone flower cart or a group of men and women parading in their best suits and dresses after Sunday morning Mass, whether vacant, rubble-strewn lots or the relentless demolition crews of urban renewal.

The Catholic Church, of course, played a major role in the life of those early migrants. Back in 1950, Holy Agony Church, then on East 98th Street, was about to be torn down by the city to make room for a public housing project. At the time, it was one of only two Catholic churches in New York—the other being the now-defunct La Milagrosa on East 115th Street—that ministered to the newly arrived Puerto Ricans. Doña Carmen Livigne, whom I met many decades later when she was in her 80s, organized a delegation to visit Cardinal Francis Spellman and urged him to build a new Holy Agony. Cardinal Spellman agreed, but only if the parish raised the money. Livigne and scores of volunteers then went door-to-door for months until they had collected enough money to convince the church hierarchy they were serious. By 1952 the new Holy Agony, built from the sacrifices of thousands of Puerto Rican blue-collar workers, opened its doors at the corner of 103rd Street and Third Avenue. For decades after that, Holy Agony became the religious soul of Puerto Rican El Barrio, and it is where my family worshipped.

When Goldstein first trained his lens on them, Puerto Ricans were still an invisible group. Sure, a small colony of migrants from that sun-drenched Caribbean island had existed in the city since the early 20th century, their number growing to about 135,000 by World War II. But most of them were concentrated in a few out-of-the-way enclaves: along the Brooklyn waterfront, in Lower Manhattan, and in South Central and East Harlem. World War II changed all that. Tens of thousands of Puerto Ricans from the island were drafted to fight in that conflict, and when those veterans returned from the front many chose to leave their homeland and head to New York. They were drawn here by unseen push-and-pull factors. Industry in the Northern states needed cheap unskilled labor, while Puerto Rico's nominally autonomous government was eager to encourage mass migration to stem social unrest among the island's impoverished masses. And since the Puerto Ricans were already U.S. citizens, there were few obstacles to their migration.

More than 40,000 came to New York in 1946 alone. My family was part of that wave. My parents, Juan and Florinda González, arrived on one of the first regular Pan American Airline flights from San Juan. They settled in a typical railroad tenement cold-water flat on East 112th Street near First Avenue, with the bathtub in the kitchen and a single toilet in the hallway that was shared by all the families on that floor.

This extraordinary exodus from the island continued without letup for two decades. By the mid 1960s, more than a million Puerto Ricans were living in the United States, largely concentrated in New York City and secondly in Chicago. In subsequent years, the migrants spread far and wide, from inner-city Boston to the farmlands of South Jersey and Connecticut, to Orlando, Florida and Houston, Texas and Anchorage, Alaska. Today, there are more people of Puerto Rican descent residing in the continental U.S. (5.1 million) than in Puerto Rico itself (3.3 million).

East Harlem has remained the cultural heart of this vast diaspora throughout all those decades. Most of the migrants who came during the 1940s and 50s spoke little English, they had only the barest education, and they worked the most menial jobs. They quietly pushed carts in the city's garment center, cleaned bedpans in its hospitals, washed dishes in its hotels and restaurants, did maintenance work for the big apartment buildings, or they worked on factory assembly lines, or drove gypsy cabs, or operated storefront bodegas. It was, in sum, a working class migration.

Yet the contradiction of being at once citizens and foreigners made the Puerto Rican experience in America an extremely complex one, especially since ours was a racially mixed population. The reigning racial biases of this country meant that black or dark-skinned Puerto Ricans faced greater ostracism, beyond those of just normal ethnic or language prejudice. This made the Puerto Rican experience different in significant ways from previous immigrants, and more akin to that of African Americans or Native Americans than to any other Latino group. The lighter-skinned among us tended to settle in more stable Italian or Irish neighborhoods, and some even passed for white. Those with darker skin, unable to find housing in white neighborhoods, formed all-Puerto Rican communities or moved into black neighborhoods, so that in many Northern cities, Puerto Rican settlements soon turned into buffer zones between blacks and whites.

Our family's building in East Harlem was located near the city-owned Jefferson Pool, smack in the middle of the Italian section of East Harlem that extended all the way to Third Avenue. At the time, most Puerto Ricans settled west of Third Avenue but the González clan managed to survive for several years on a largely Italian block only because my Aunt Pura had married an Italian whose family owned the grocery store downstairs.

Undoubtedly, it also helped that my aunt performed volunteer work in the office of the legendary congressman from East Harlem, Vito Marcantonio. An old-style socialist, Marcantonio had spent years fashioning a unique coalition of Harlem's Italians, Puerto Ricans, and African Americans. That coalition kept him in congress from 1934 to 1950, when an alliance of the city's mainstream political parties finally united behind one candidate to defeat him. With Marcantonio gone, East Harlem lost its main voice for working class unity. Racial tensions flared up immediately, as some Italians blamed Puerto Ricans for his defeat. Young ethnic gangs that had started to form in the late 1940s became more common, with each group defending its own territory from incursions by the others. Whenever an African-American or Puerto Rican youth dared to try to swim in the Jefferson Pool, for instance, racial clashes inevitably erupted.

Soon, the tabloid newspapers began fueling hysterical stereotypes of Puerto Rican criminals as savages. The most notorious early examples were Frank Santana and Salvador "Capeman" Agron. Santana garnered front-page headlines in 1955, when, as a teenage gang member, he murdered a white boy and was sentenced to life in prison. Four years later, Agron was captured following a sensational manhunt, and subsequently convicted for the fatal stabbing of two white youths during a gang fight in Hell's Kitchen. Agron was sentenced to the electric chair until a social movement in the Puerto Rican community convinced Governor Nelson Rockefeller in 1962 to commute his sentence to life in prison.

By then, Hollywood producers had begun producing a spate of films that fashioned the enduring image in the American psyche of Puerto Ricans as knife wielders, prone to violence and addicted to drugs. Such films included *Cry Tough* (1959), *The Young Savages* (1961), and *West Side Story* (1961). The media and Hollywood narratives were soon buttressed by a slew of academics, among them the anthropologist Oscar Lewis, who propounded theories of a trans-generational "culture of poverty" among Puerto Ricans in books like *La Vida,* which won Lewis the National Book Award in 1967. But by then, the children of that first generation of Puerto Rican migrants, like myself, had grown up. Some of us had finished high school, a few even gotten through college.

We instantly rebelled against the racist narrative that Puerto Ricans had become a problem for U.S. society. We had seen our parents work themselves to death to ensure a better life for us, despite their facing constant hostility. We had seen the city and the country prosper from their labor. We quickly became part of the broad Civil Rights protest movement of 1960s. In groups like the Young Lords, the Black Panthers, and El Comité, young Puerto Ricans forced major government reforms in housing, health care, and education policies for racial minorities. We even spawned our own group of activist photographers, people like Frank Espada, Hiram Maristany, and Michael Abramson, who chronicled in their work militant and bold new images of East Harlem and of Puerto Rican life in America. But long before Frank or Hiram or Michael, we now know that there was Leo Goldstein, a solitary photo artist of the 1950s who trained his lens on this heroic but little-known community of migrants seeking to realize their hopes and dreams in one small neighborhood of this nation's greatest city. We who lived through those years in East Harlem can assure you, his lens was truer than any of the news articles, movies, or books of the era, and we are all enriched by the work he left behind.

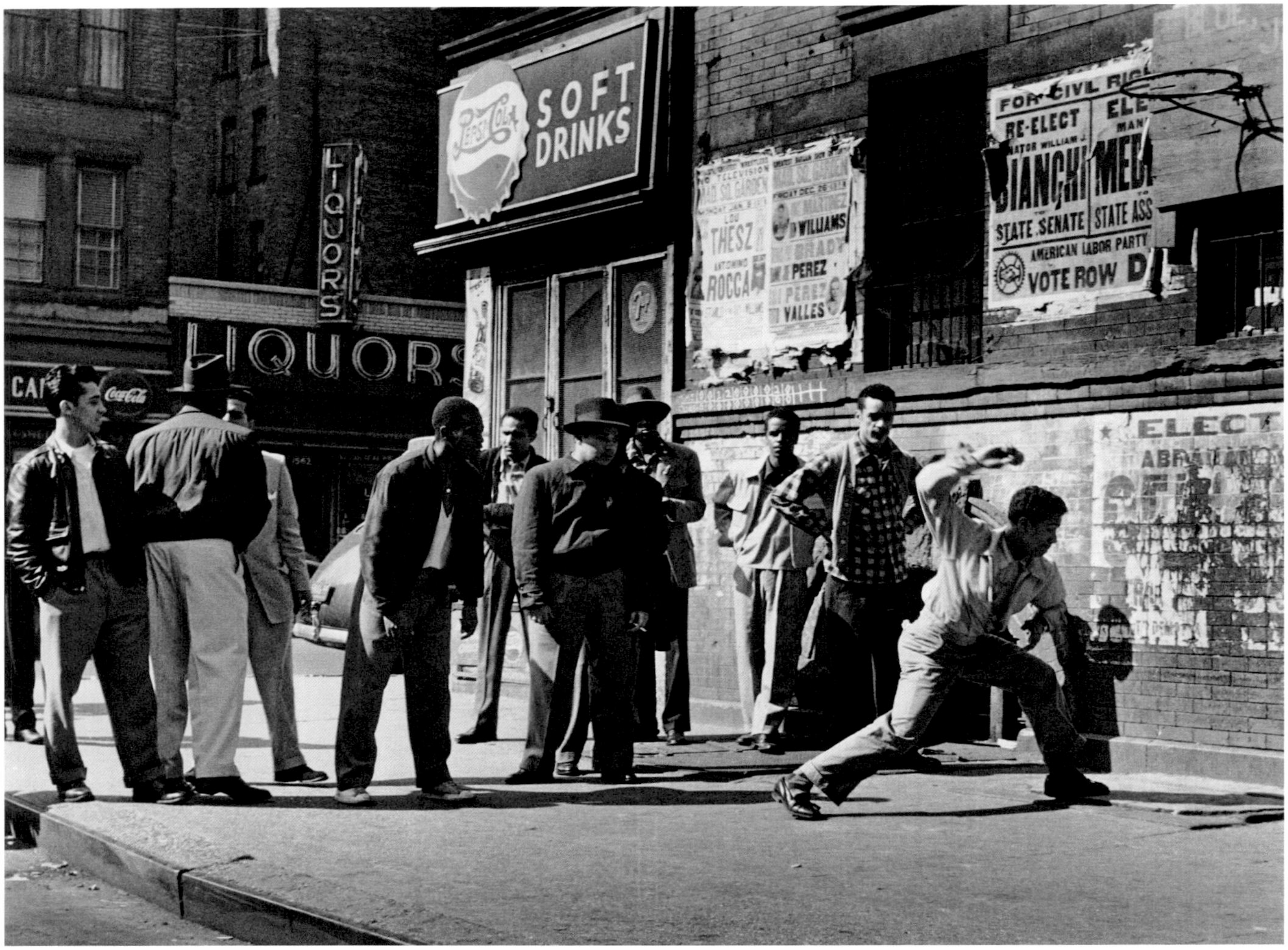

Playing ball, c.1952

Leo Goldstein in East Harlem by A. D. Coleman

When in 1949 Leo Goldstein stepped with his used Rolleiflex twin-lens reflex camera onto the streets of what would eventually become known as Spanish Harlem, he couldn't have imagined that he would become an intriguing footnote in the history of photography.

Known then as East Harlem, and eventually called "El Barrio" ("The Neighborhood") by its Spanish-speaking residents, this section of Manhattan stretches approximately from the north side of East 96th Street up to East 142nd Street, and from the east side of Fifth Avenue all the way to the East and Harlem Rivers. Starting in the 1860s, it absorbed influxes of immigrants from Ireland, Germany, and various Nordic and eastern European nations, most of whom had moved upward and out by the end of World War II. At the time Goldstein began his work there, this run-down but affordable district had become a magnet for working-class Latinx and Hispanic immigrants—mostly from Puerto Rico, but also from Cuba, Mexico, the Dominican Republic, and other Latin American countries—who clustered within its boundaries in the postwar years.[1]

Goldstein shared their immigrant status, if not their ethnicity; born in 1901 in Czarist Russia, he had come to America and New York City in 1906 when his family fled the pogroms. Though they had moved elsewhere (during the period in which he made these photographs Leo resided on West 83rd Street), the Goldstein family had lived for a time in East Harlem, on East 117th Street and then East 119th, so he was hardly a stranger to this neighborhood. No less importantly, he came from the same economic class as its then-current residents, and had experienced a comparable dislocation—geographic, cultural, and linguistic—in his childhood transplantation from Russia. Moreover, as a worker himself and a committed leftist (even at the outset of the McCarthy era and the "Red Scare") Goldstein surely felt himself in solidarity with everyone oppressed and scrabbling to survive in his home city.

How he came to photograph in East Harlem specifically remains unclear. Most likely it resulted from a combination of Goldstein's familiarity with its streets and his seriousness of purpose as an avocational photographer, the latter of which resulted from his involvement in the now-famous Photo League, a short-lived, pioneering organization based in New York City. This connection requires some context.

Goldstein came to his interest in photography at a time when the now-expansive post-secondary photo-education system had barely begun. If you lived in or near Rochester, in upstate New York, you could enroll in the Kodak-subsidized program at the Rochester Institute of Technology, basically a feeder system for the photo-manufacturing industry. In the Chicago area you could study at the Institute of Design, in a program established there by the Hungarian émigré László Moholy-Nagy, who had devised it for the Weimar Bauhaus and transplanted it (and himself) to the U.S. at the outset of World War II. A few other schools around the country offered courses in the medium, most of which emphasized the various applied functions of the medium: product photography, studio portraiture, architectural and scientific usages, and so forth.

Outside of such limited options, available primarily to enrollees in college-level institutions, people who wanted to learn how to take pictures with their cameras came to the medium along a variety of less formal paths: apprenticeship; trial-and-error, in conjunction with the already plentiful manuals and periodicals aimed at the amateur market; the occasional independent workshop taught by figures like Ansel Adams and Minor White; and the instruction and facilities available at the nearest camera club.

Camera clubs have all but vanished from the scene, both nationally and internationally, but at least through the middle 1960s they played an important yet still under-recognized role in both the education of photographers and what you might call their socialization, by which I mean their induction into a local, regional, national, and even international network of people—mostly but not exclusively male and white—who shared a common interest in the medium. Large cities would have several, but even small towns might have one. This constellation of organizations had emerged in the late 19th century, solidified in the early years of the 20th, become respectable and influential by the 1930s and through the war years, then began to fade away, in large part because the kinds of imagery this tutorial system encouraged had become deeply conservative and outmoded.

Still, camera clubs in the late 1940s represented one of the few situations in which you could walk in off the street with your new or second-hand camera and no experience whatsoever and find people who, at little or no expense, would teach you how to use it—and also how to develop your own film and make your own prints in the club's darkroom, even critiquing your results according to their standards, however fusty.[2] For many professionals in the field, these organizations served as their entry point.

The Photo League originated in New York City in 1930, at the outset of the Great Depression. A forthrightly left-wing version of the then traditional camera club, it emphasized social-documentary work—not the exclusive concern of its programs and membership, but heavily weighted in that direction—photography's version of social realism. That made it entirely untypical in terms of content and attitude; in effect, its founders adapted the infrastructure of the camera-club model to the politics and interests of its members. Unique among such organizations not only in the New York City area but nationwide, it exerted a disproportionate influence still felt today.[3]

Goldstein joined the Photo League in the late 1940s, almost two decades after its initial formation as the Worker's Camera League and—this shows his commitment and courage—a year or so after U.S. Attorney General Tom C. Clark formally declared the League subversive and placed it on the U.S. Department of Justice blacklist in 1947. That meant Goldstein's involvement in the League lasted just a year or so before it closed down in 1951, though former members, Goldstein among them, continued to meet informally thereafter to pursue privately their mutual interests in the medium.

The timing suggests that Goldstein could have crossed paths with such now-legendary League members as Paul Strand, Ralph Steiner, Berenice Abbott, Sol Libsohn, Sid Grossman (who served as director of the Photo League School), Walter Rosenblum, Eliot Elisofon, Morris Engel, Jerome Liebling, Aaron Siskind, Dan Weiner, Lou Bernstein, Arthur Leipzig, Louis Stettner, Lisette Model, and Ruth Orkin. Other notables who, though not members, participated in the League's activities in one way or another included Margaret Bourke-White, W. Eugene Smith, Helen Levitt, Arthur Rothstein, Beaumont Newhall, Nancy Newhall, Richard Avedon, Weegee, Robert Frank, Harold Feinstein, Ansel Adams, Edward Weston, and Minor White. The League also housed the Lewis Hine Memorial Collection, and took Hine (1874–1940) and his predecessor, the muckraking journalist Jacob Riis (1849–1914) as their guiding spirits. One can hardly imagine a more fertile intellectual and creative environment for an emerging photographer.

The group engaged in several collective projects, in particular the "Harlem Document" project (1936–41) involving a "Feature Group" of ten photographers led by Aaron Siskind. While this preceded Goldstein's membership in the League, and resulted in no publication at the time, prints and notes from the project surely resided in the organization's files, and the underlying concept—a respectful, empathetic exploration of a marginalized and often maligned ethnic group concentrated in a specific neighborhood—may well have served as a model for whatever Goldstein and others undertook in East Harlem, which in turn functions as counterpoint to the better-known survey.

Goldstein left no written memoir or recorded oral history of his experiences with the group and its members, unfortunately. And almost all of the above-named luminaries have passed on. Evidence indicates that Goldstein knew and was close to Strand, and on occasion photographed side by side with Rosenblum. But, unless and until other documentation comes to light, we can only guess as to which of the others affected him directly.[4]

However, we can make some of those guesses in an educated way. Though it seems an unlikely marriage, in terms of printmaking strategies the League had adopted the "purist" approach of the then-ascendant, avowedly apolitical West Coast-based Group f/64. That cluster of photographers—Ansel Adams and Edward Weston most prominent among them—advocated a "straight" or unmanipulated print, with a full tonal range, made directly from the original negative and interpreted by the maker of said negative, as the only way to achieve the full realization of the photographer's individual vision or "way of seeing."

Radical at the time, especially in contrast to the often manipulated and otherwise highly stylized approaches to printmaking promulgated by the still-prominent pictorialist movement and prevalent in the camera-club environment, this set of negative-control and printmaking guidelines seemed to suit the concerns of these East Coast social documentarians. None of Goldstein's negatives have survived.[5] But, looking at the consistently exhibition-quality prints he left as his legacy, we can see that someone, presumably at the League, taught him to make just such prints, their richness and luminosity enhanced by his choice of a medium-format camera, whose larger negative encodes more data about both the subject and the light bouncing off that subject than the smaller 35mm camera increasingly popular for such work at the time.[6]

Goldstein's use of the medium-format Rolleiflex has another, less immediately visible effect on his pictures. On the one hand, it's small enough not to seem obtrusive or draw attention to itself. On the other hand, one can't operate it as rapidly as one can a 35mm rangefinder camera (such as the Leica); it doesn't lend itself to furtive grab-shooting of the kind we commonly associate with "street photography." As we can see from Goldstein's images, he made himself known to those he photographed, planted himself in front of them, and offered them the empowering opportunity to control their own self-presentation in the collaborative making of these transactional environmental portraits.

Furthermore, the user holds such a camera, most commonly, at waist level, looking down at the image in the ground glass.[7] As a consequence, the lens looks slightly upward at most full-grown human subjects, rather than straight at or down at them; it engages children head-on. This has a psychological effect, first of all on the subject (it's less confrontational) and subsequently on the image, and, through that, on the viewer; looking up at someone from a lower position registers in a much different way, perhaps especially when the simulated experience of direct eye contact gets added,[8] as in most of Goldstein's portraits.

And, in these pictures, Goldstein comes across as, above all, a portraitist. While he shows us aspects of the quotidian street life of East Harlem in that era (workers at a construction site, players and spectators at a stickball game, a family coming back from the market), Goldstein places his emphasis on direct engagement with the area's residents, treating them not as types but as individuals described with loving attention to detail, collectively comprising a vibrant sector of the city and a notable component of its population largely ignored—indeed, almost invisible to all but its members.

So Leo Goldstein's gift to us comes as a densely packed time capsule describing one of New York City's many microcultures at mid-century, a very particular historical moment in the life of a vital but largely overlooked community.[9] It takes the form of a substantial, carefully redacted body of work, defining itself as such by dint of the fact that Goldstein himself picked these negatives to print so carefully. His family's decision to preserve this archive for all these years, and now to make it public for the first time, delivers an experience akin to finding a single case of a fine rum from a vintage year and a distillery previously unknown and no longer in operation. Seven decades later, we have only to recognize its rarity, acknowledge its quality, give thanks for its survival against the odds, and savor it.

ENDNOTES

1 For a literary chronicle of the experiences of this community, I recommend Jesús Colón's *A Puerto Rican in New York and Other Sketches* (New York: Mainstream Publishers, 1961; second edition, New York: International Publishers, 1982). Colón (1901–1974) emigrated to the U.S. in 1917. This book collects the cream of his writings as published in the U.S. Communist Party newspaper *Daily Worker*; that column, which Colón initiated in 1955, describes this community pretty much as Goldstein found it a few years earlier. An inspiration to other writers of the same background, this book, and Colón's other writings, seeded what would later emerge as the "Nuyorican Movement." For a biography of Colón, see https://www.peoplesworld.org/article/jesus-colon-a-puerto-rican-in-new-york/.

2 The largest national organization of such clubs at the time was the Photographic Society of America. For more on the PSA, see https://psa-photo.org/index.php?about-history-of-psa.

3 For more on this organization, see Anne Tucker, *This Was the Photo League: Compassion and the Camera from the Depression to the Cold War* (New York: Stephen Daiter Gallery and John Cleary Gallery, 2001); and Mason Klein, *The Radical Camera: New York's Photo League*, 1936–1951 (New Haven: Yale University Press, 2011).

4 Nor do we know much about how Goldstein affected others. The friendship with Strand, however, led to that photographer recommending Goldstein to a publisher for a later documentation of architectural elements of New York buildings. This certainly suggests that Goldstein had earned Strand's professional respect.

5 The negatives themselves—along with any contact sheets and work prints he may have made of these images—have long since disappeared, probably discarded after his death when his basement darkroom got cleared out. The set of master prints from which the images in the present volume have been selected and the reproductions made represent all that remains of his project.

6 The following anecdote indicates that Edward Steichen, the curator of photography at the Museum of Modern Art, knew and admired some of Goldstein's work. According to Goldstein's family, he—like Harold Feinstein—turned down an invitation to participate in Steichen's 1953 blockbuster exhibition, *The Family of Man*, and for the same reason: Having absorbed the precept that a photographer's vision manifested itself most authentically in prints he or she hand-crafted, Goldstein refused to allow Steichen and his team to use his negatives to size, crop, and print his images to their own satisfaction. (That was a requirement for participation in this monumental show.) Toward the end of his life, Feinstein, in conversation with this author and elsewhere, had second thoughts about that decision. Goldstein may have felt the same, admirable as one might find the principled position underlying it.

7 The image in the viewfinder appears "right side up" but inverted left to right.

8 For an insightful overview of this effect, see Christian Jarrett, "Why meeting another's gaze is so powerful," BBC Future, January 8, 2019, http://www.bbc.com/future/story/20190108-why-meeting-anothers-gaze-is-so-powerful. Because the photographic image functions as a simulacrum of its subject(s), our responses to the human presence therein echo our responses to real-life in-person encounters.

9 In the late 1960s Bruce Davidson would photograph at length in Spanish Harlem, using a large-format camera, resulting in a controversial exhibition and book titled *East 100th Street*. For my response thereto, see A. D. Coleman, "Two Critics Look at Davidson's *East 100th Street*—What Does It Imply?" *New York Times*, October 11, 1970, p. D21.

Plates

Captions in italics reflect titles and information from the artist.

24 Three generations, c. 1950

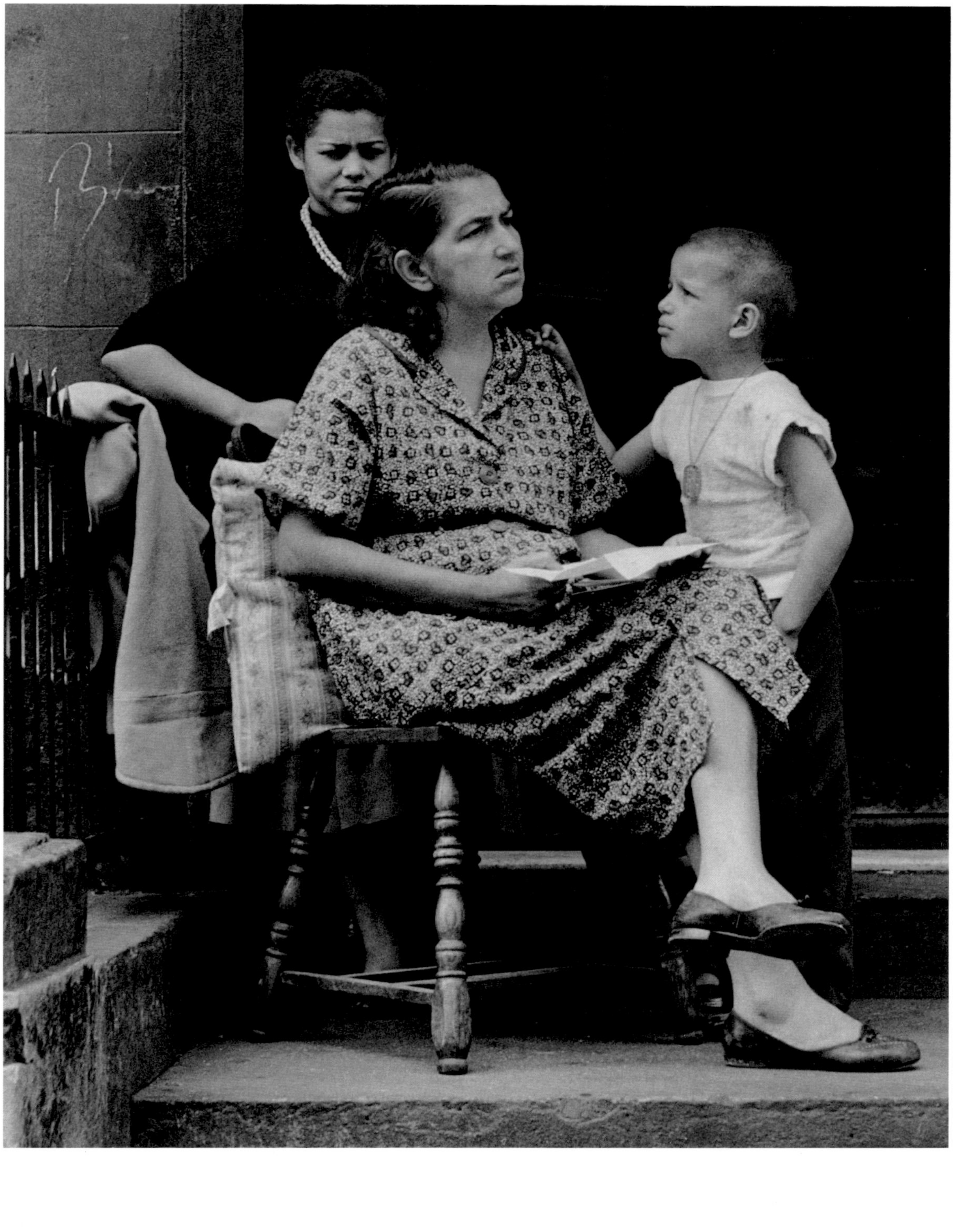

26 Girl on fence, c. 1950

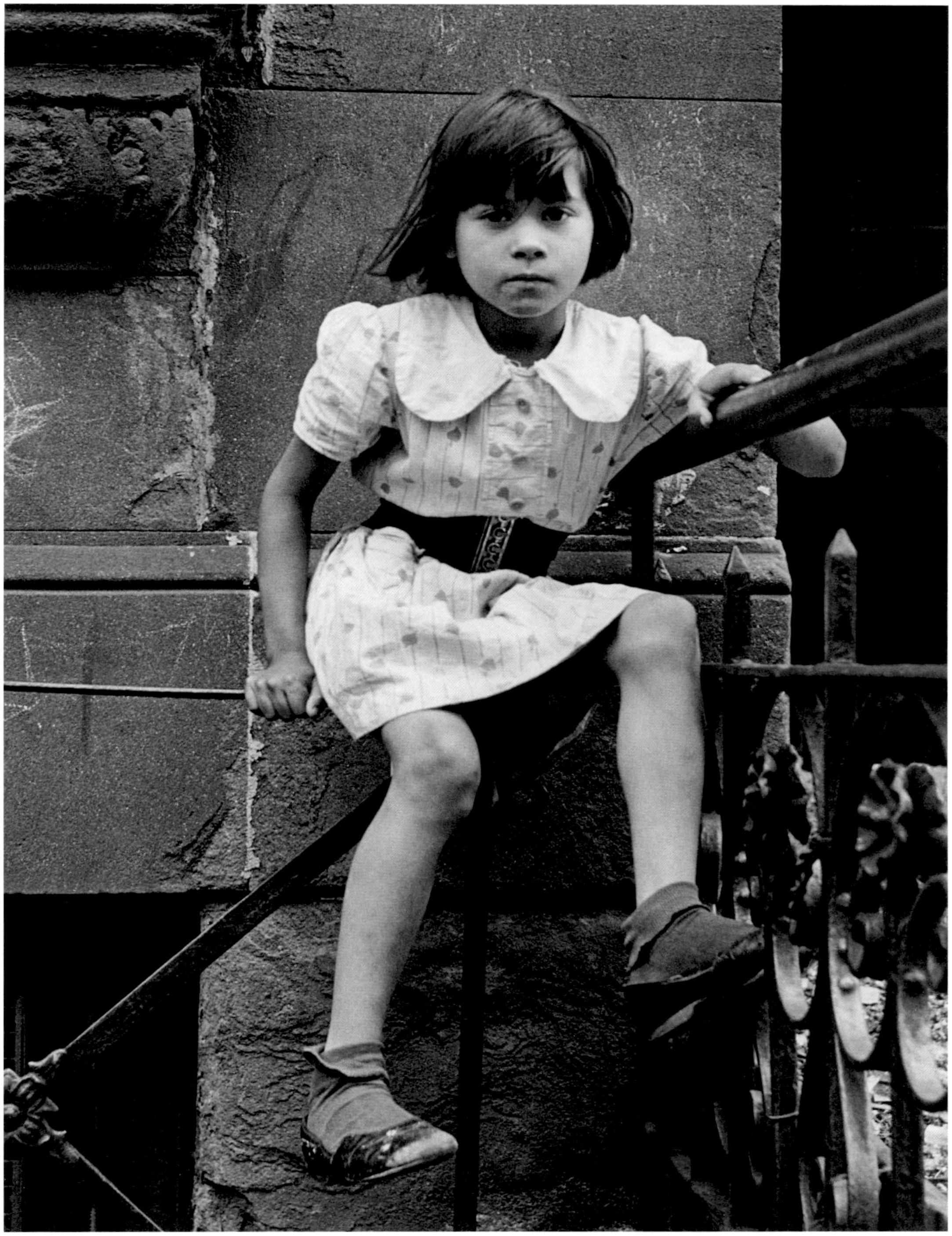

28 Three young men, c. 1950

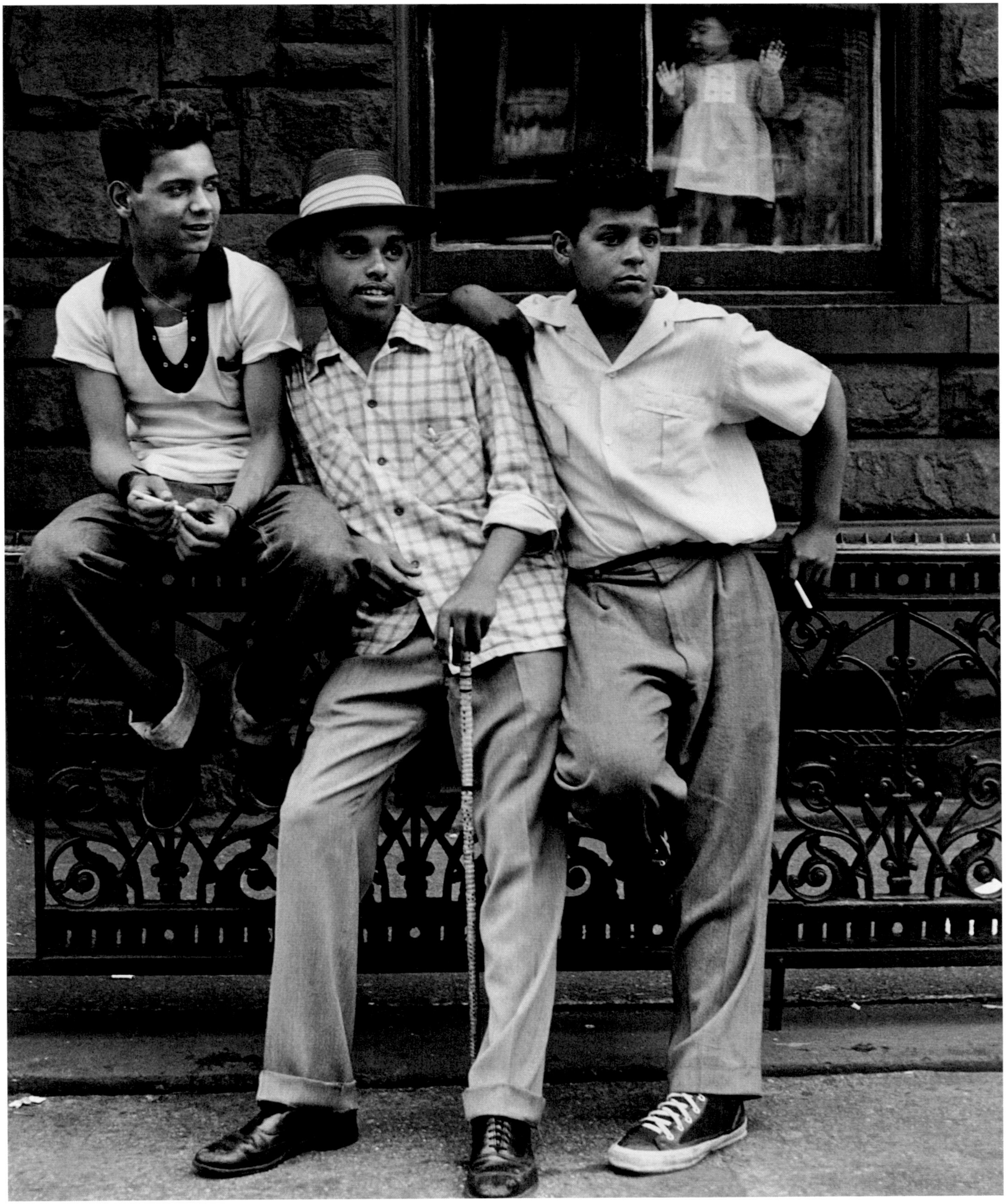

30 Girl with crying child, c. 1950

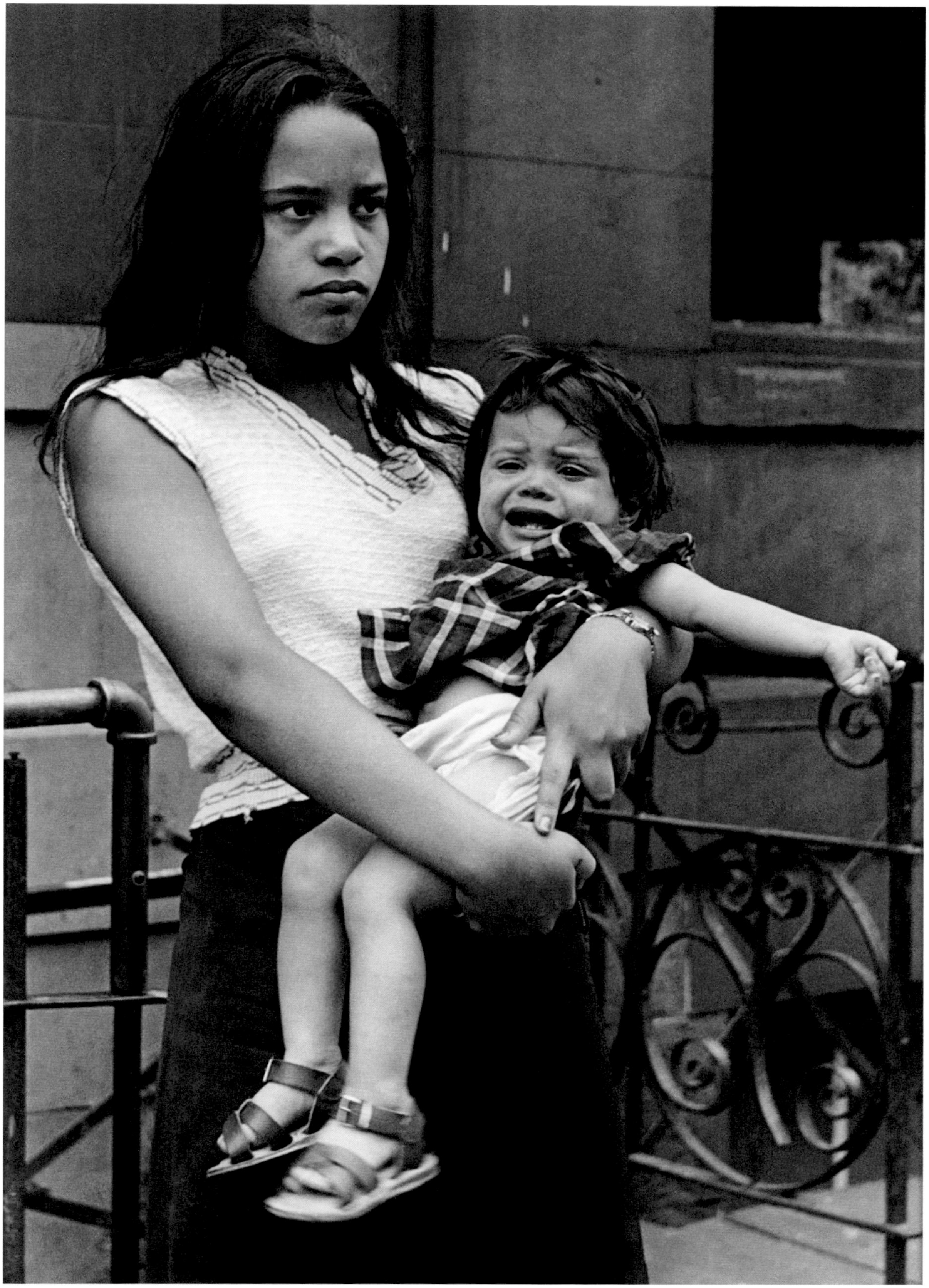

Young men on stoop, c. 1950

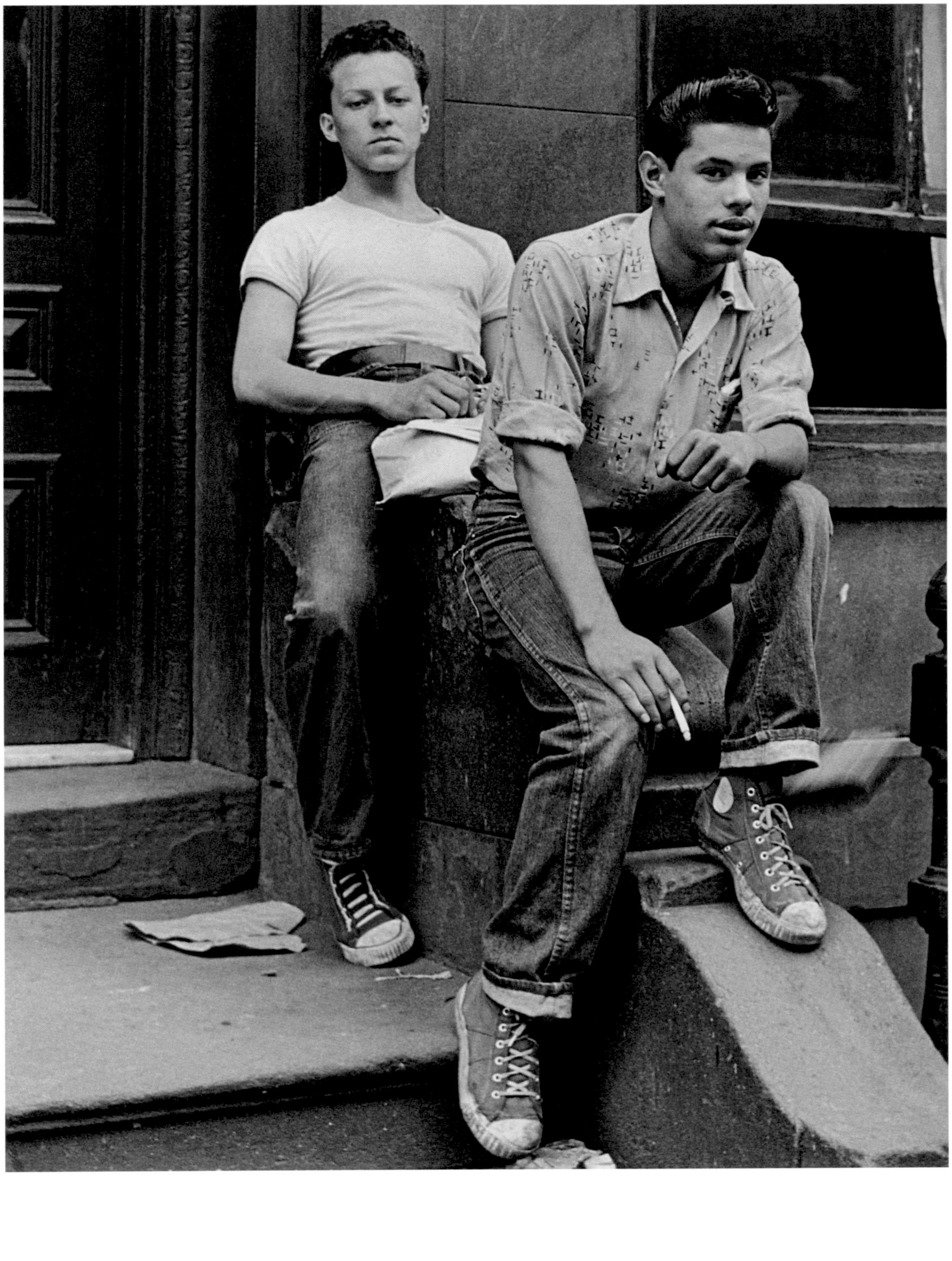

Girls on fence, c. 1955

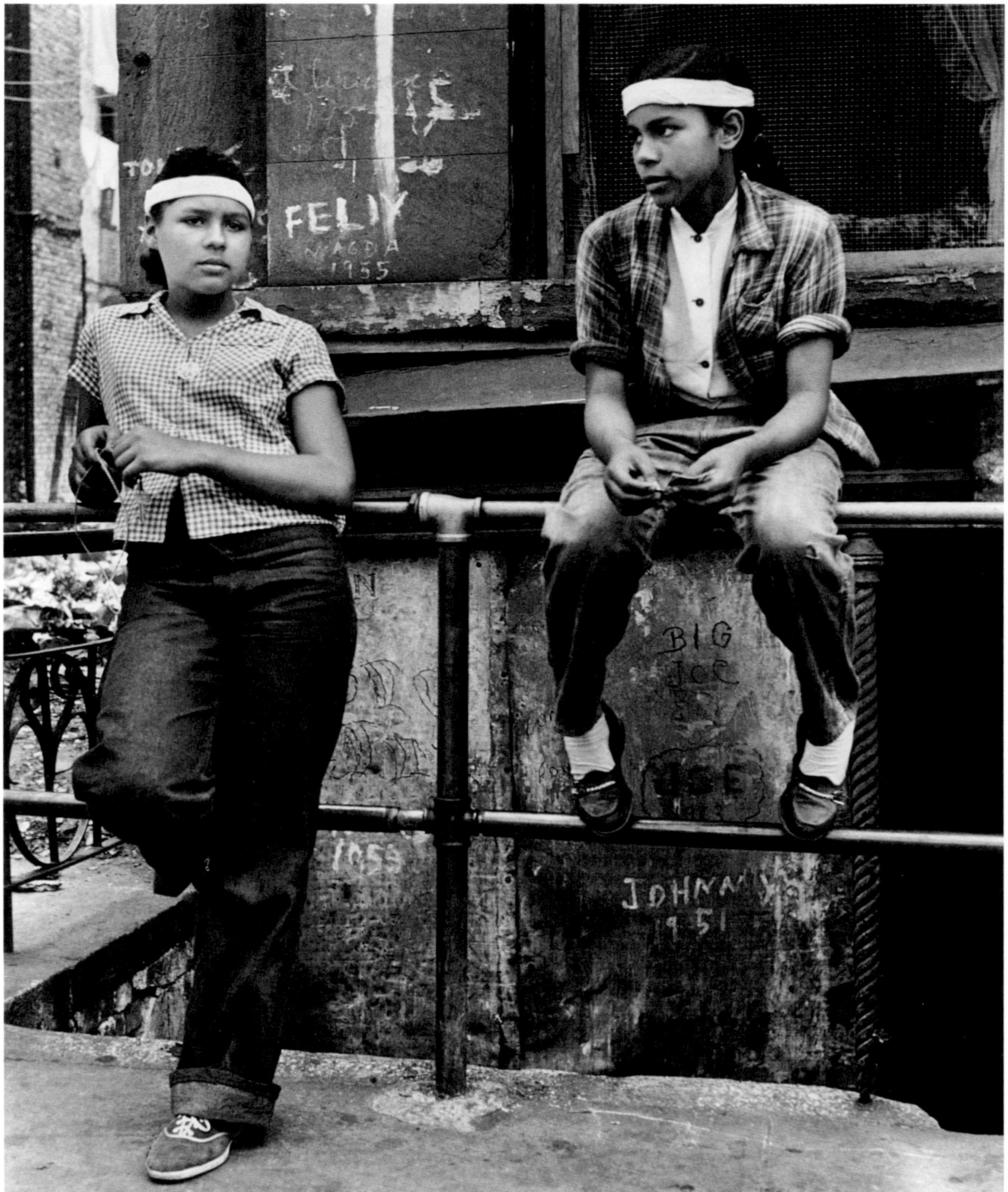
MAGDA
1955
BIG
JOHNNY
1951

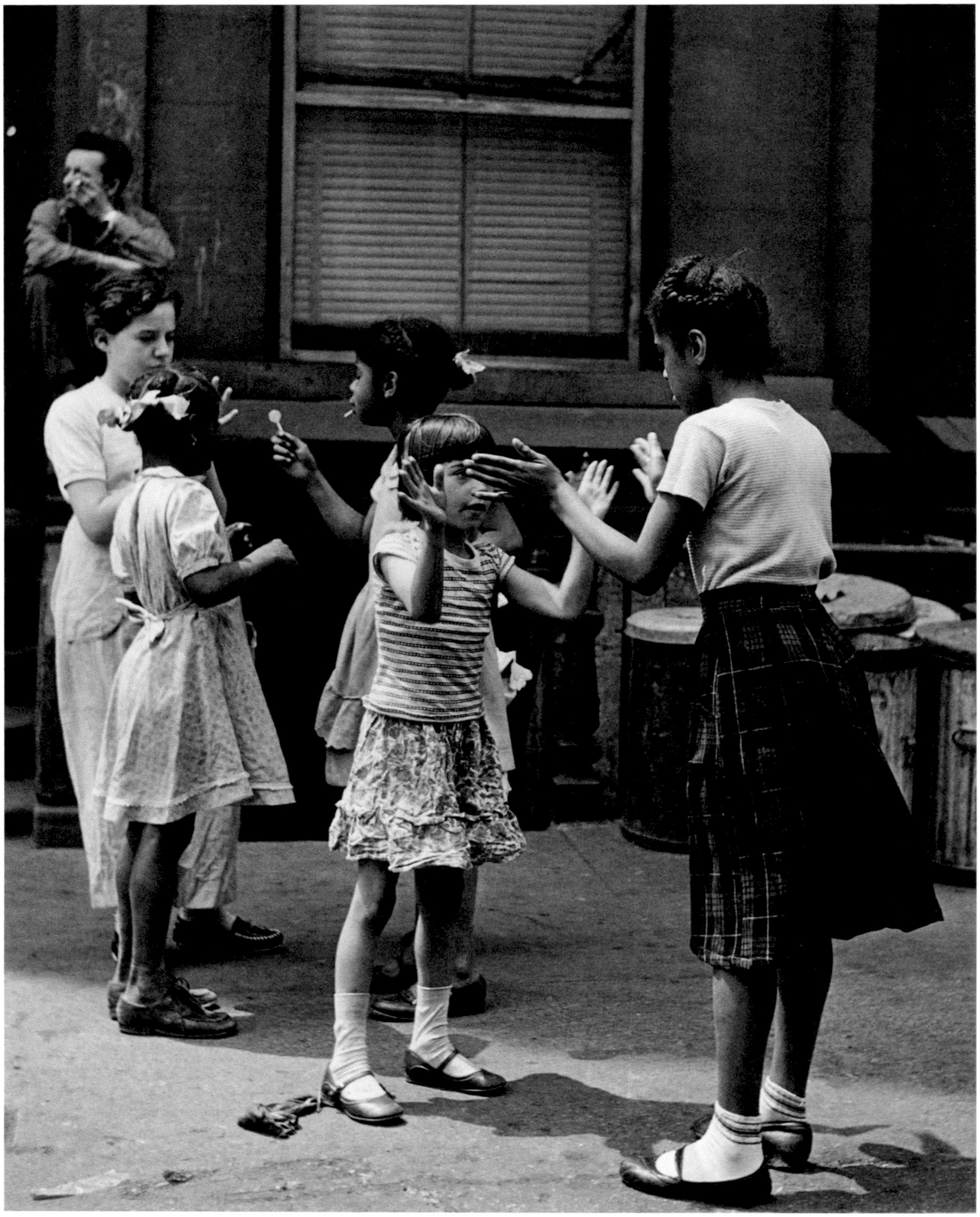

 Girl in baby carriage, c. 1950

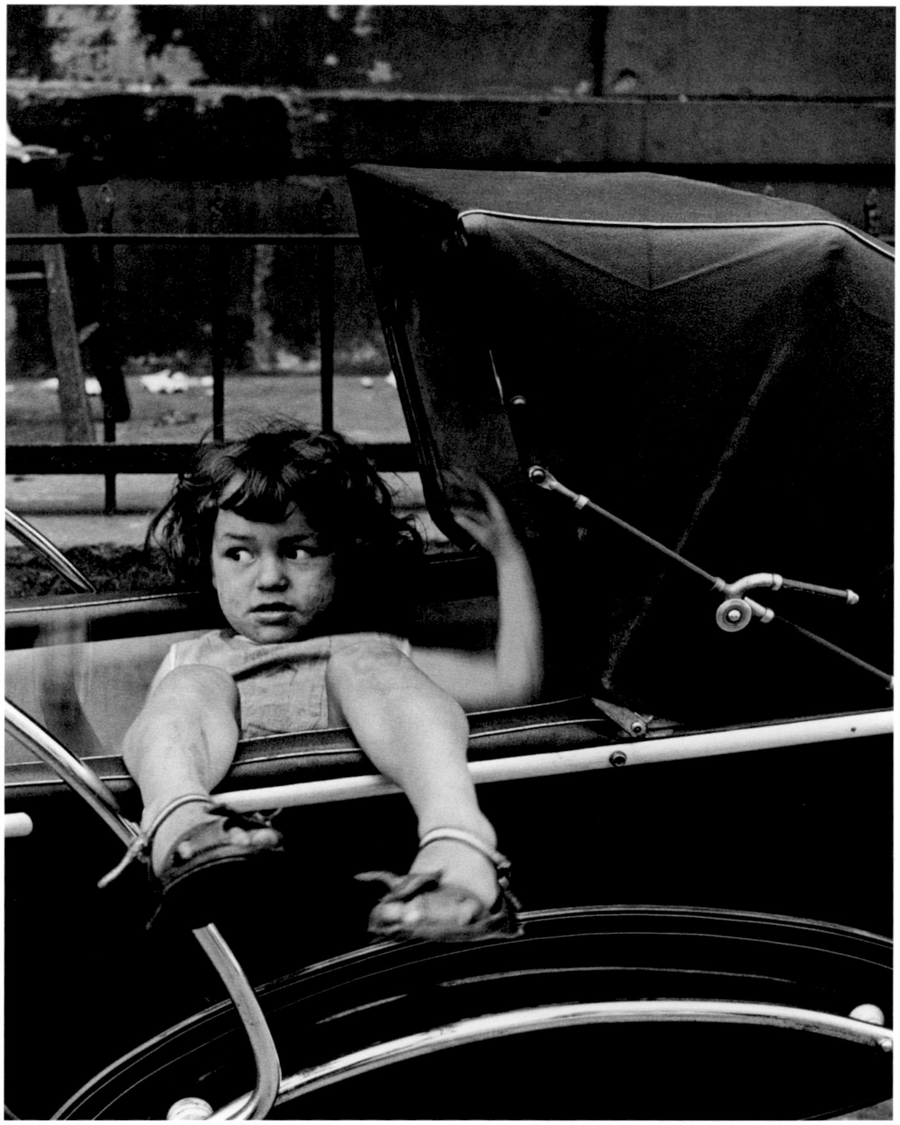

East 107th Street, c. 1955

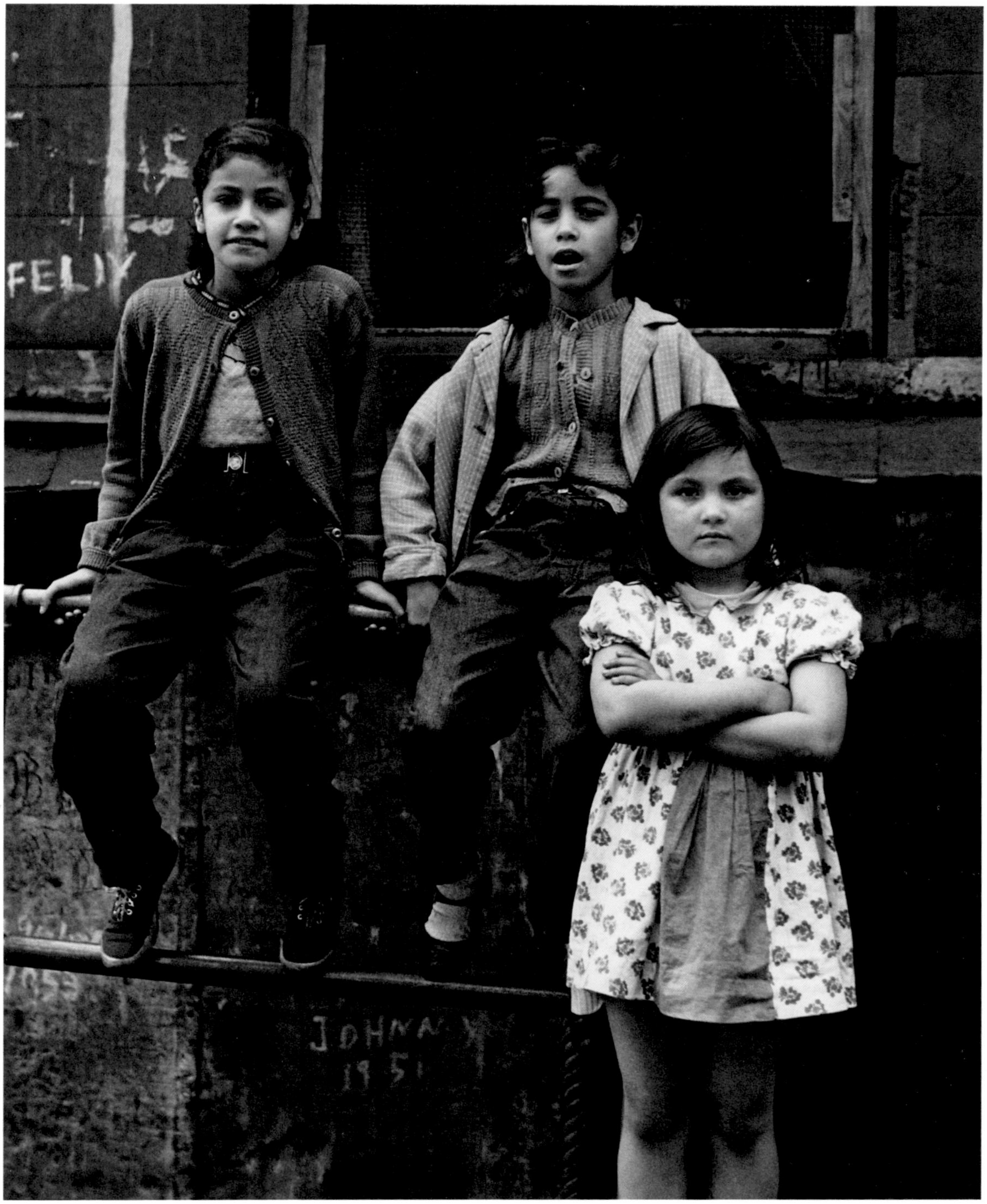

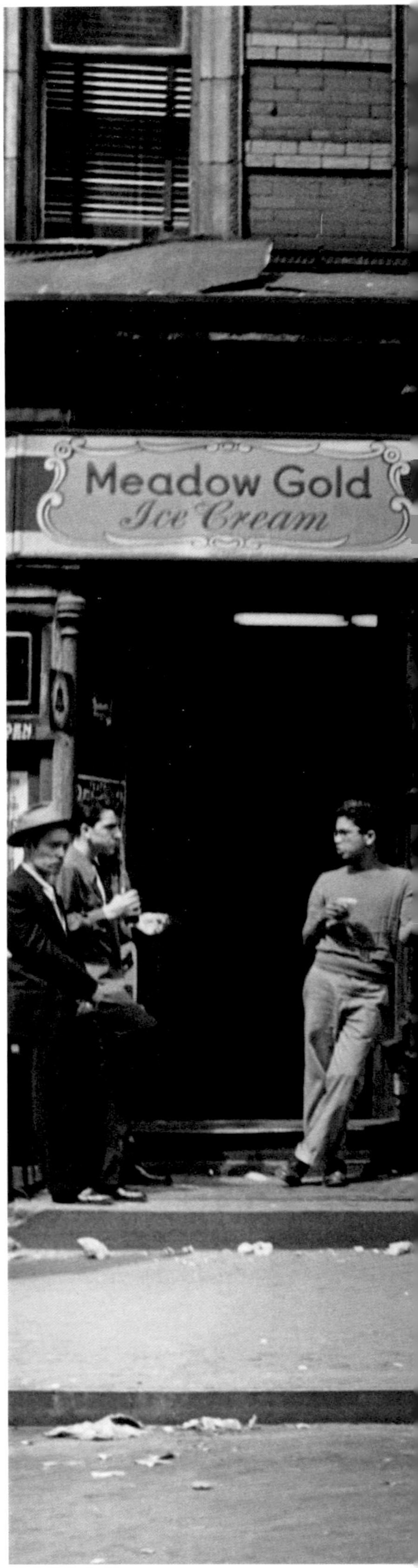

East 102nd Street (Watching a stickball game), 1951

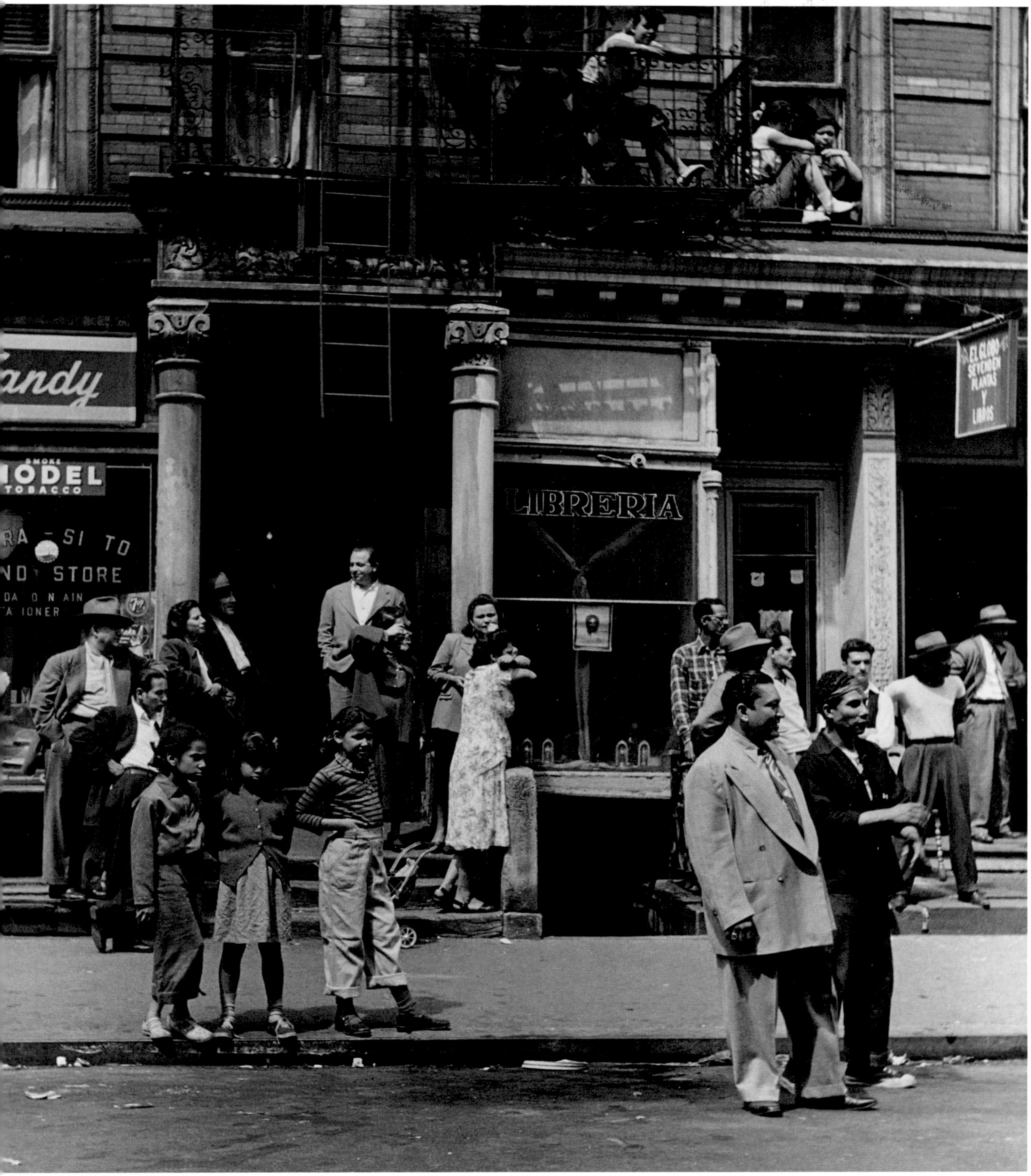
andy
ODEL
TOBACCO
STORE
LIBRERIA
EL GLOBO
SE VENDEN
PLANTAS
Y
LIBROS

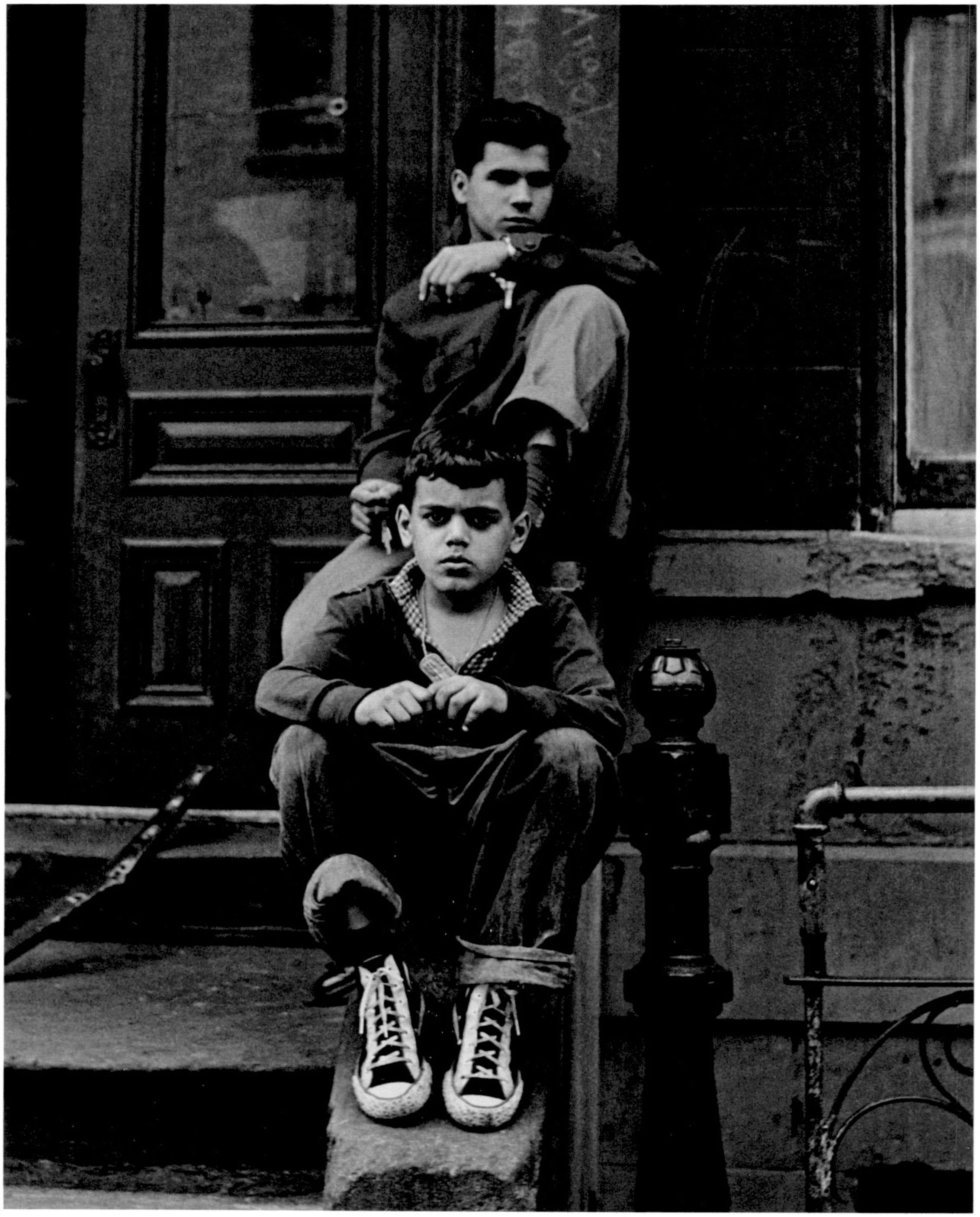

Two friends on the stoop, c. 1950

Mother and child in window, c. 1950

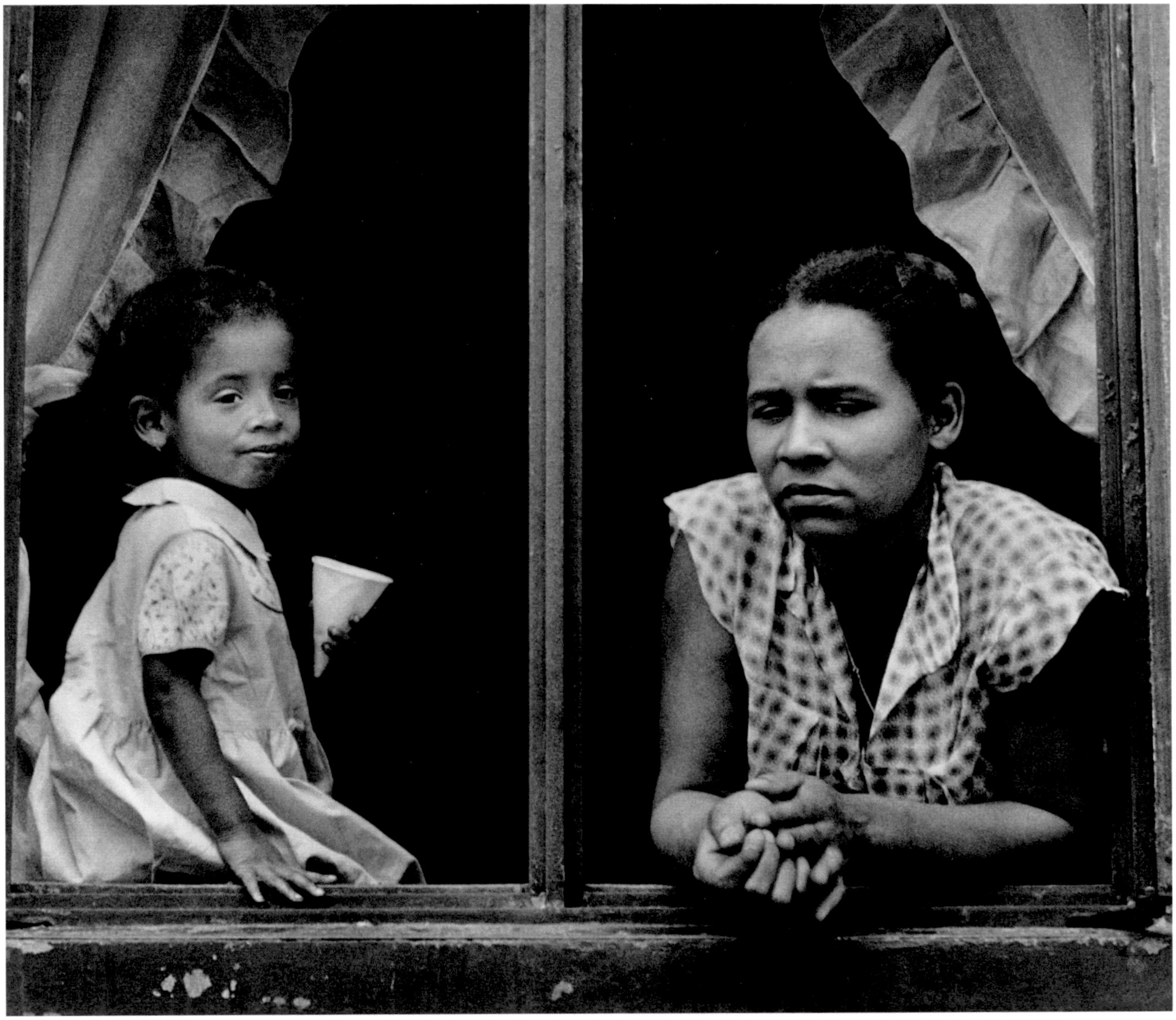

48 Girl in communion dress, c. 1950

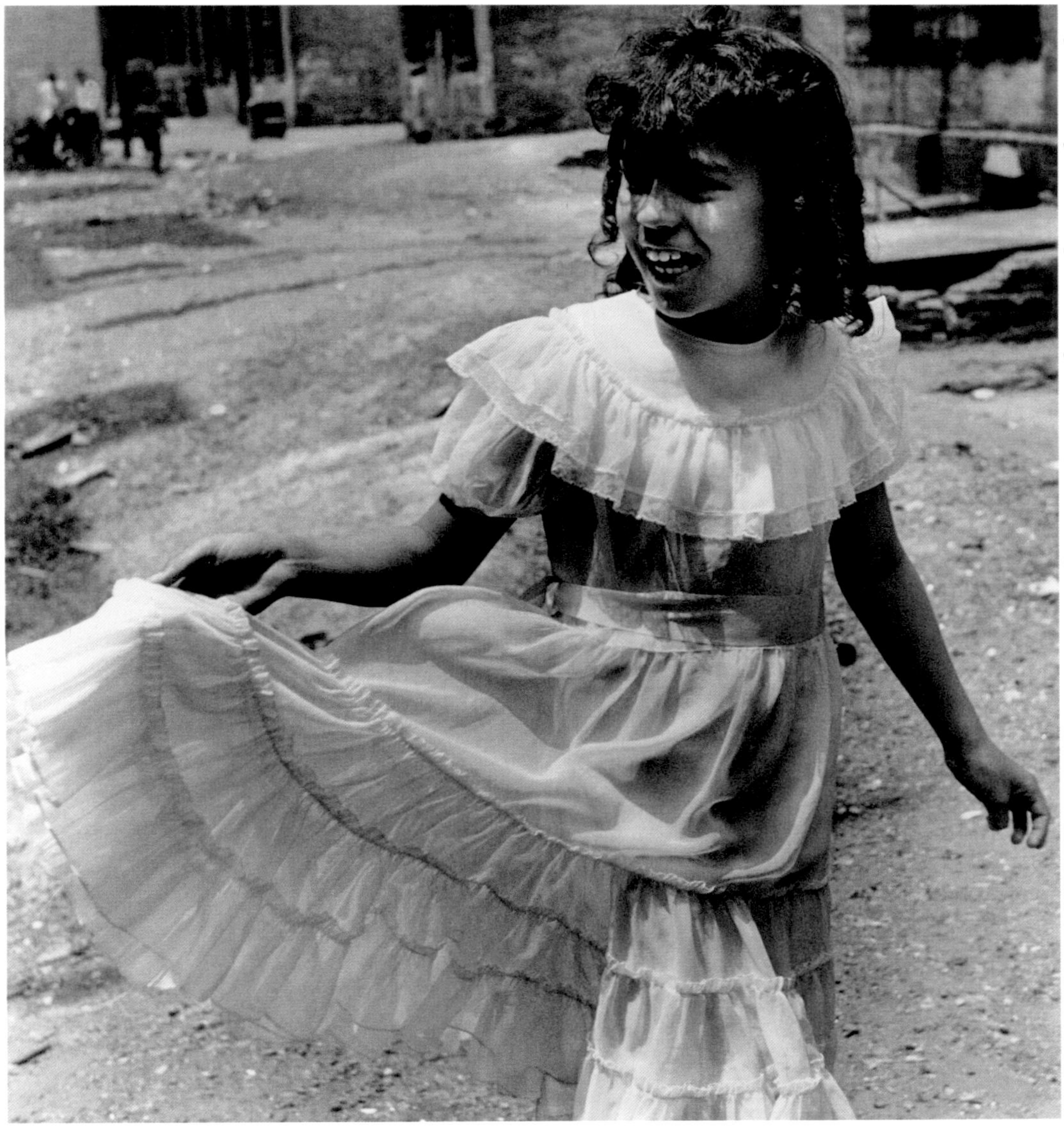

50 Boy playing clarinet, c. 1950

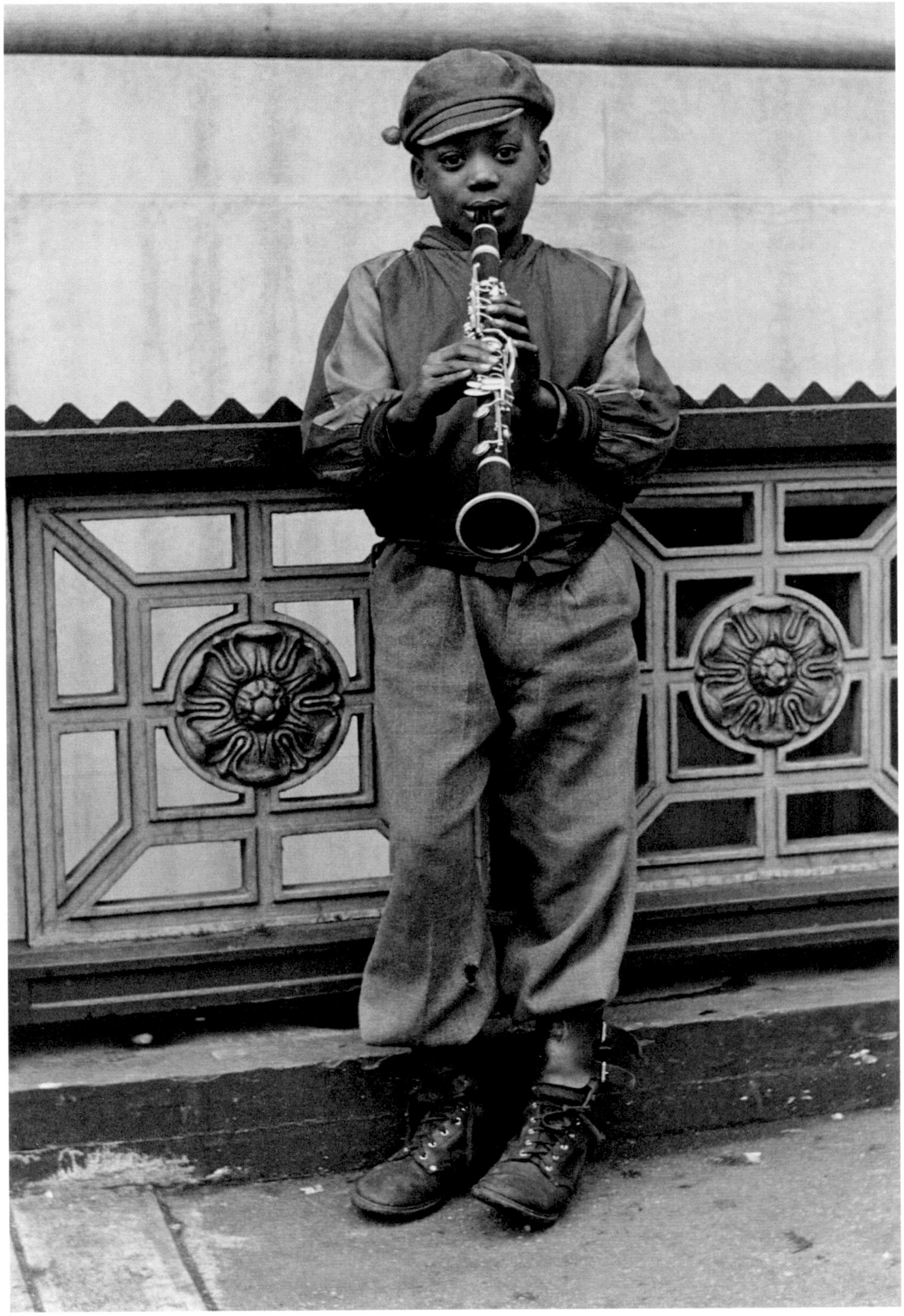

 Boys and women, Sunday, East 102nd Street, c. 1950

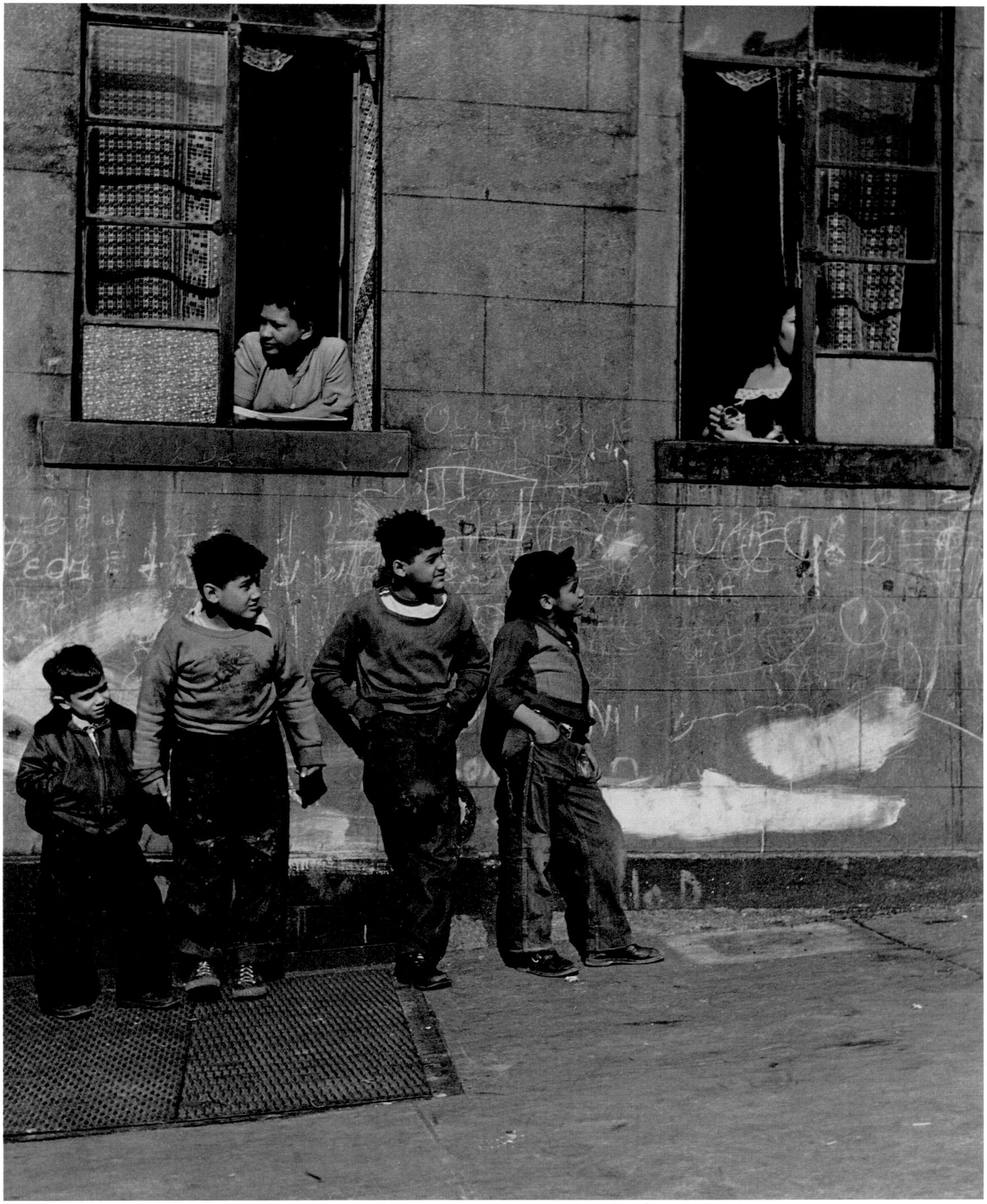

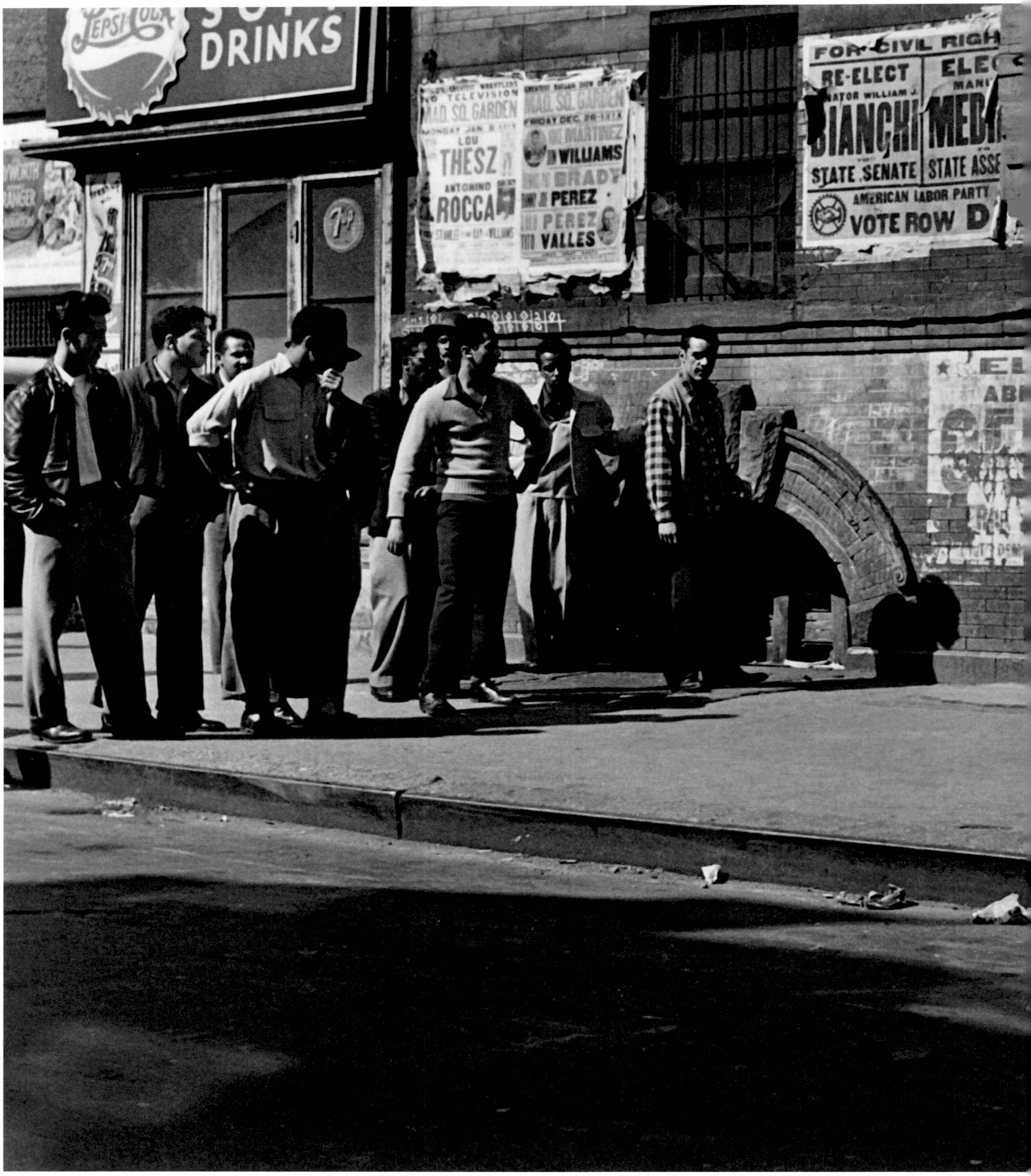

DRINKS
MAD. SQ. GARDEN
LOU
THESZ
ANTONINO
ROCCA
MAD. SQ. GARDEN
WILLIAMS
BRADY
PEREZ
VALLES
RE-ELECT
BIANCHI
STATE SENATE
AMERICAN LABOR PARTY
VOTE ROW

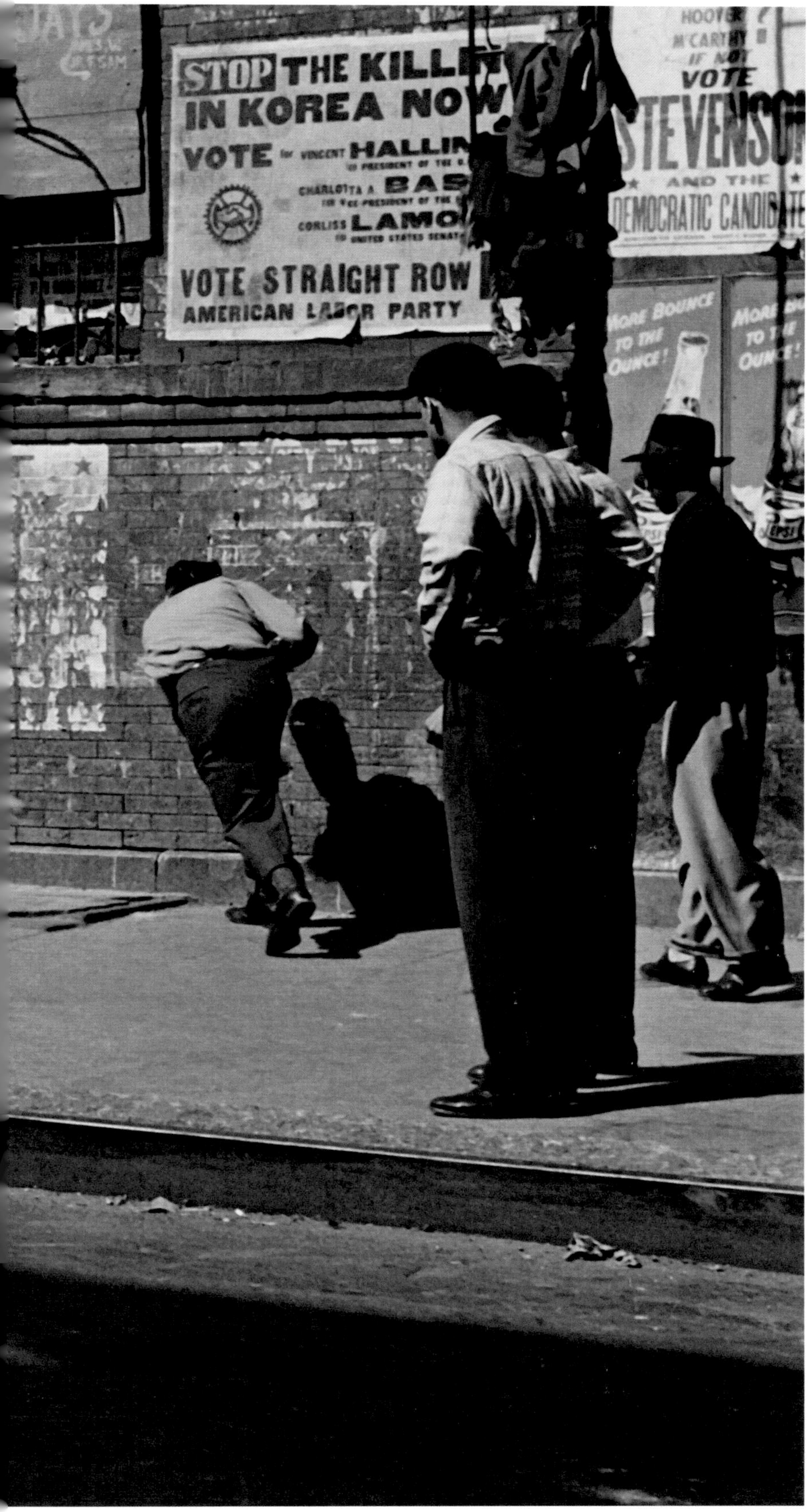

Playing ball, c. 1952

56 Injured veteran and neighbors, c. 1951

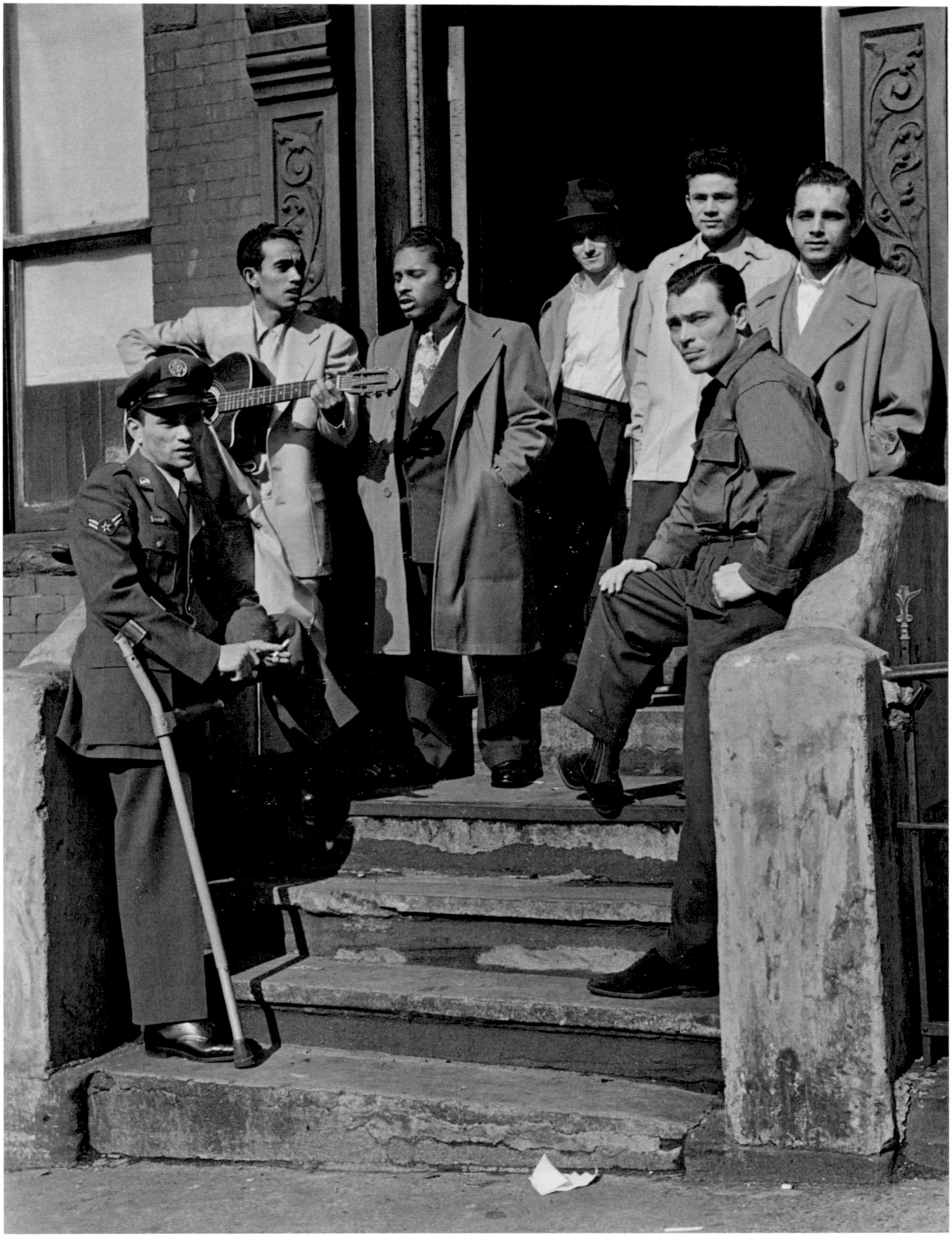

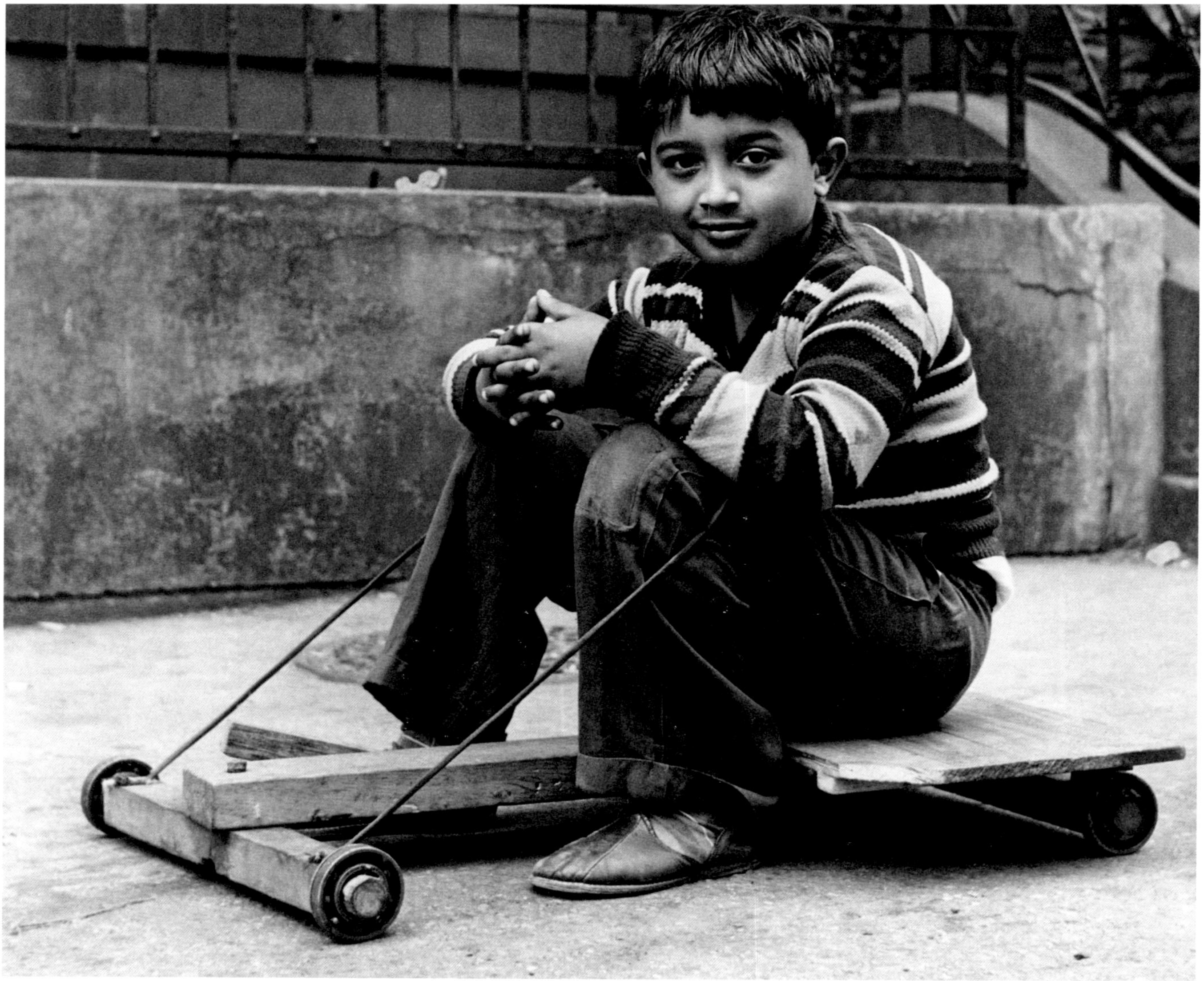

Homemade scooter, c. 1950

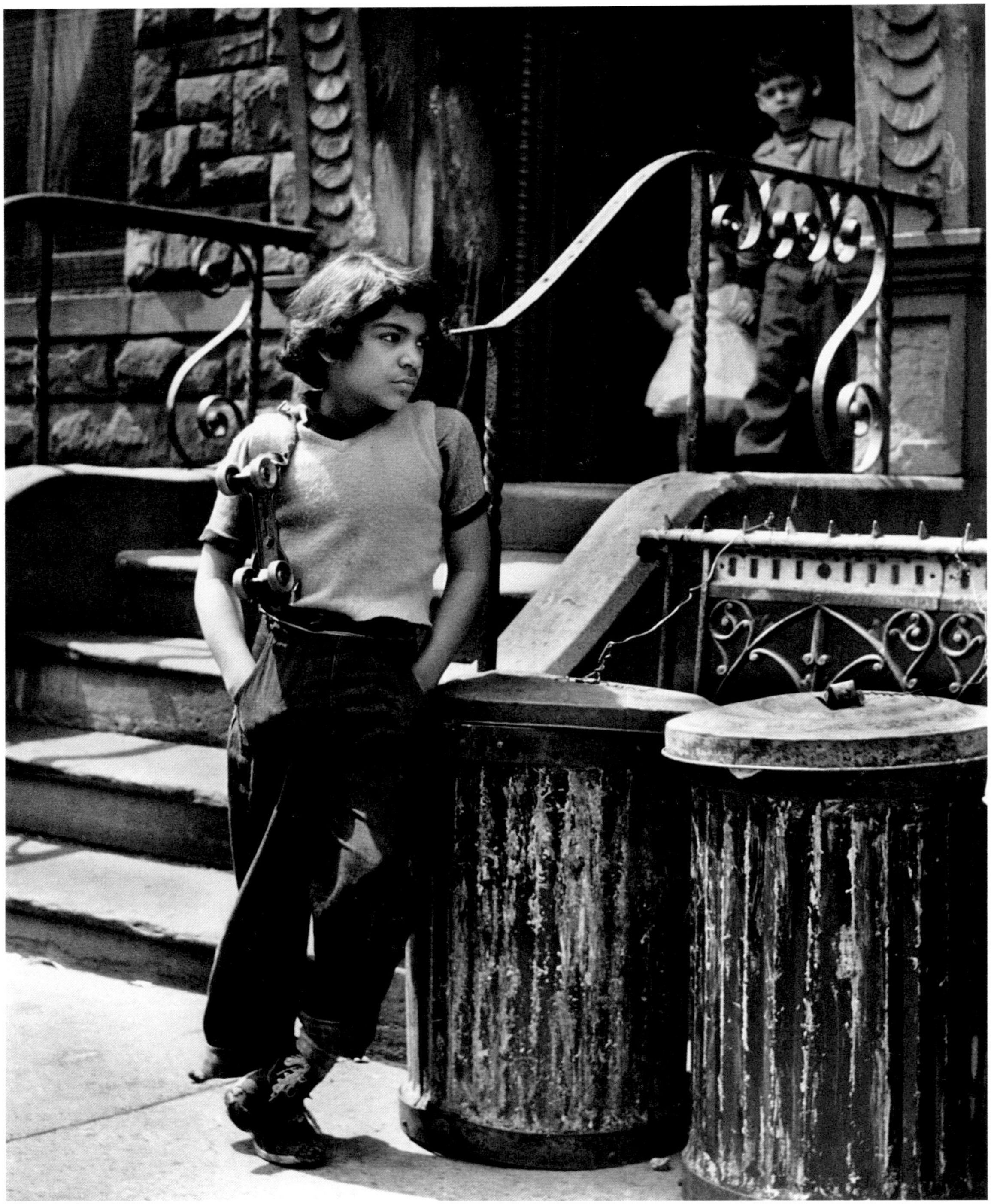

 Boy with skates, c. 1950

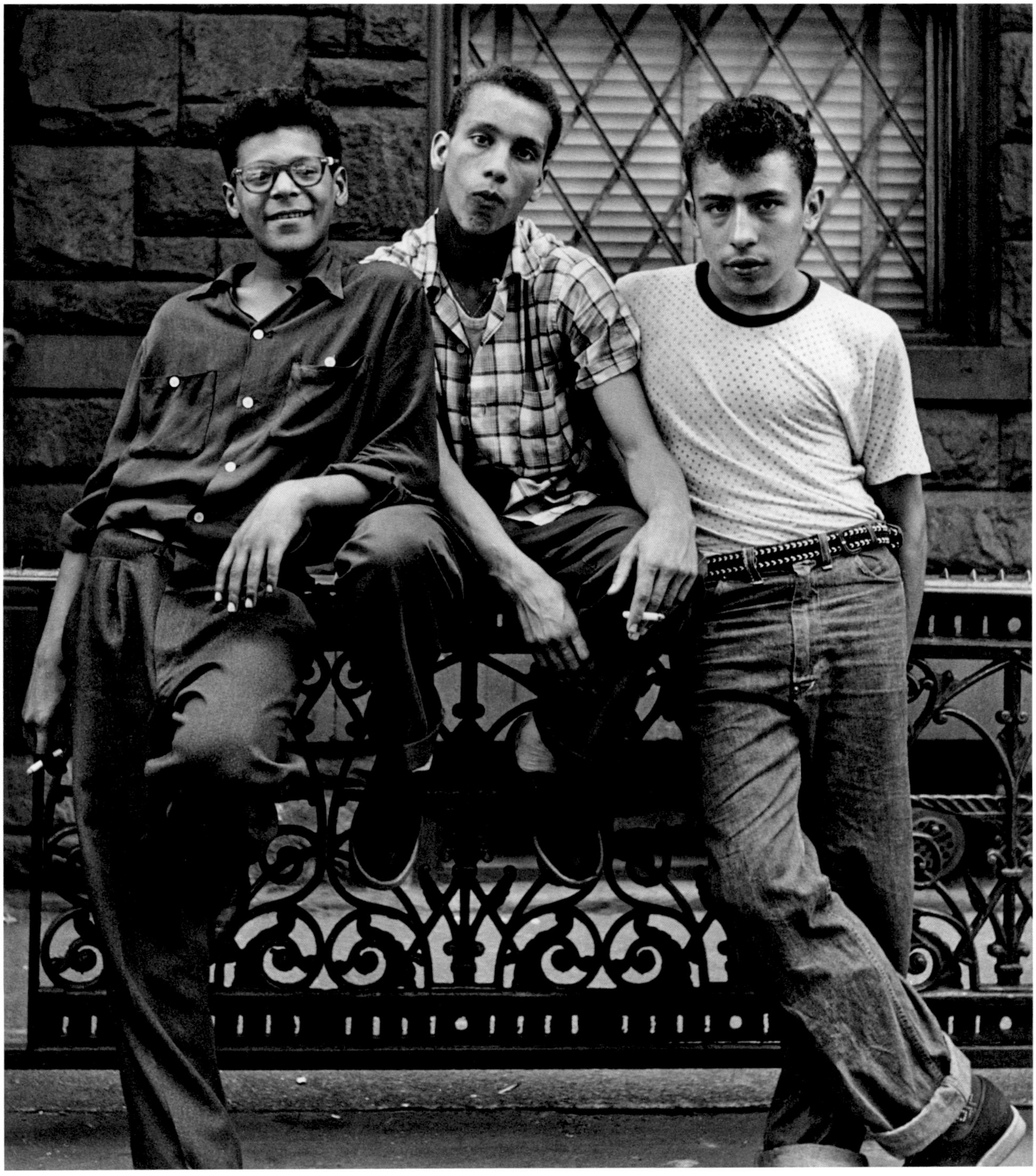

Mugging for the camera, c. 1950

Homework, c. 1950

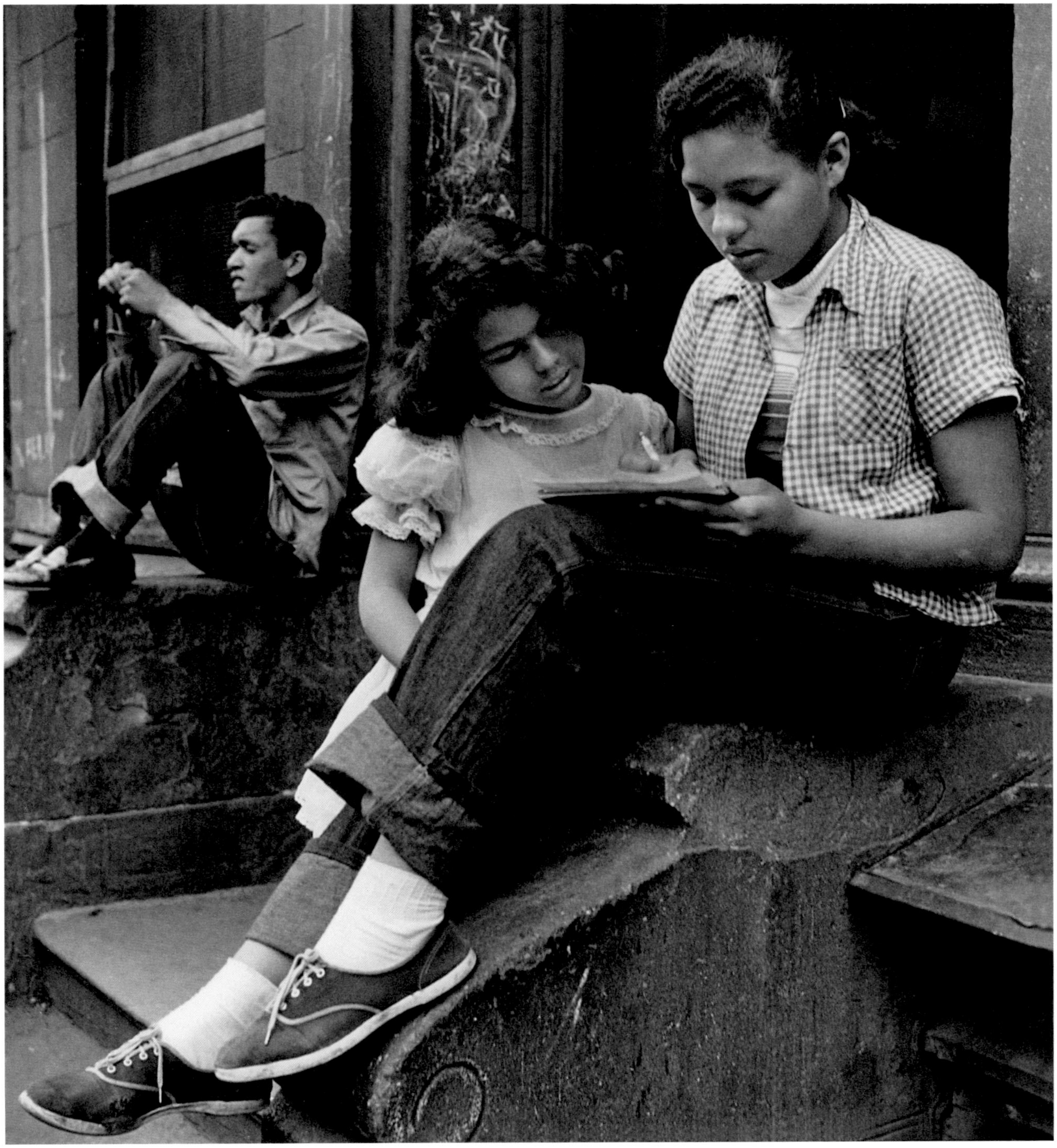

Gathering on stoop, c. 1950

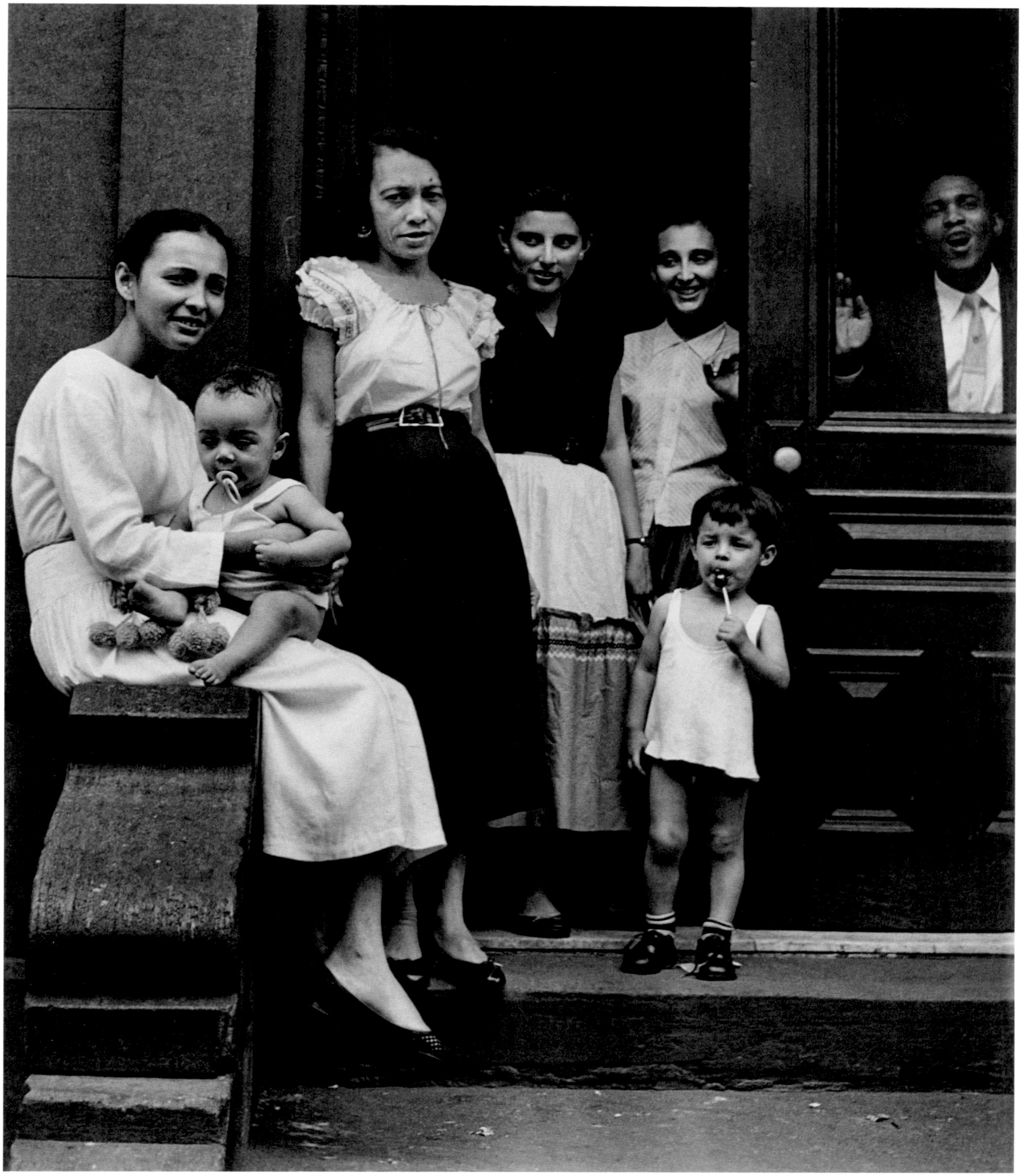

66 Portrait of two women, c. 1950

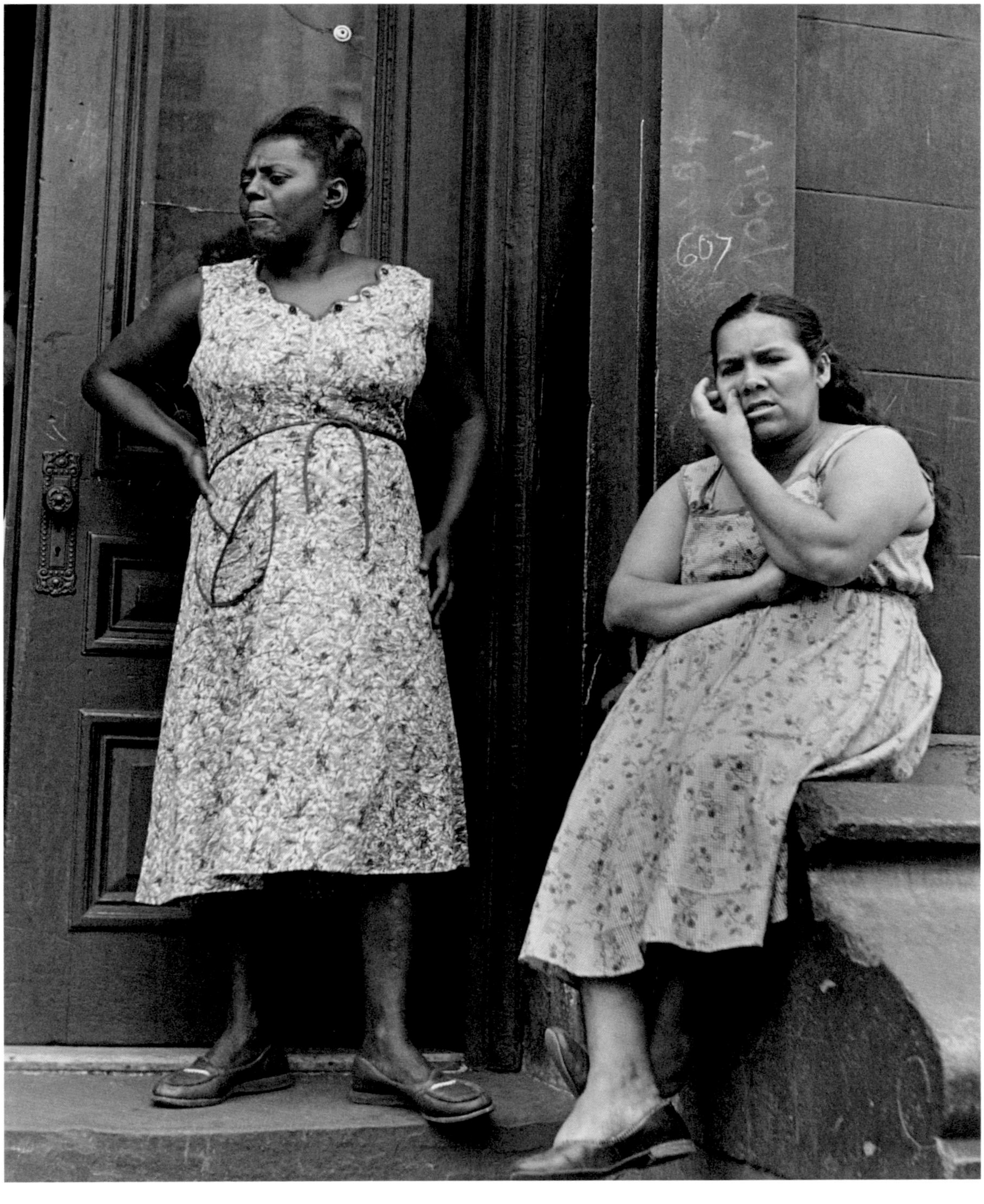
607

 Playing tops, c. 1950

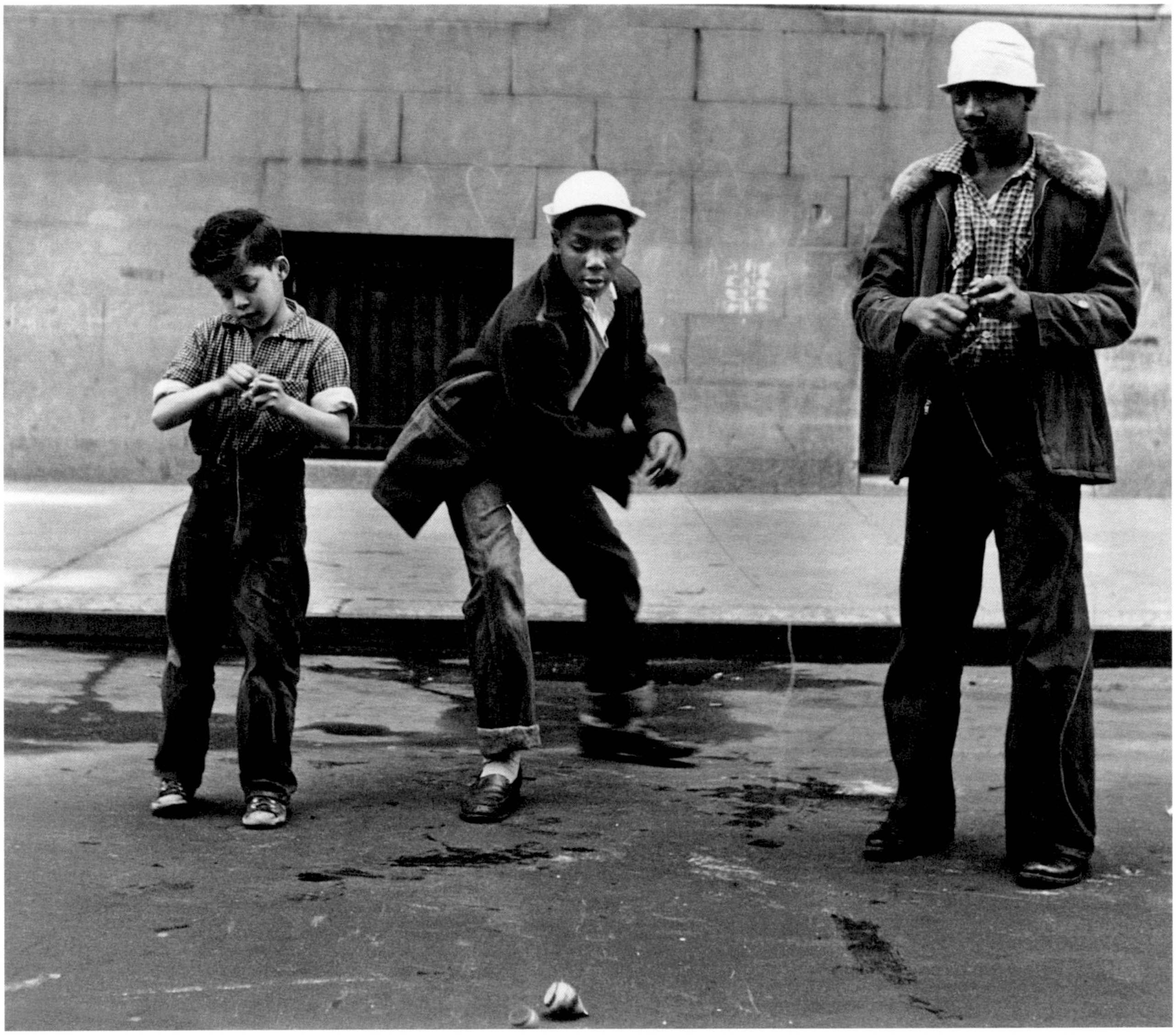

East Harlem child, 1949

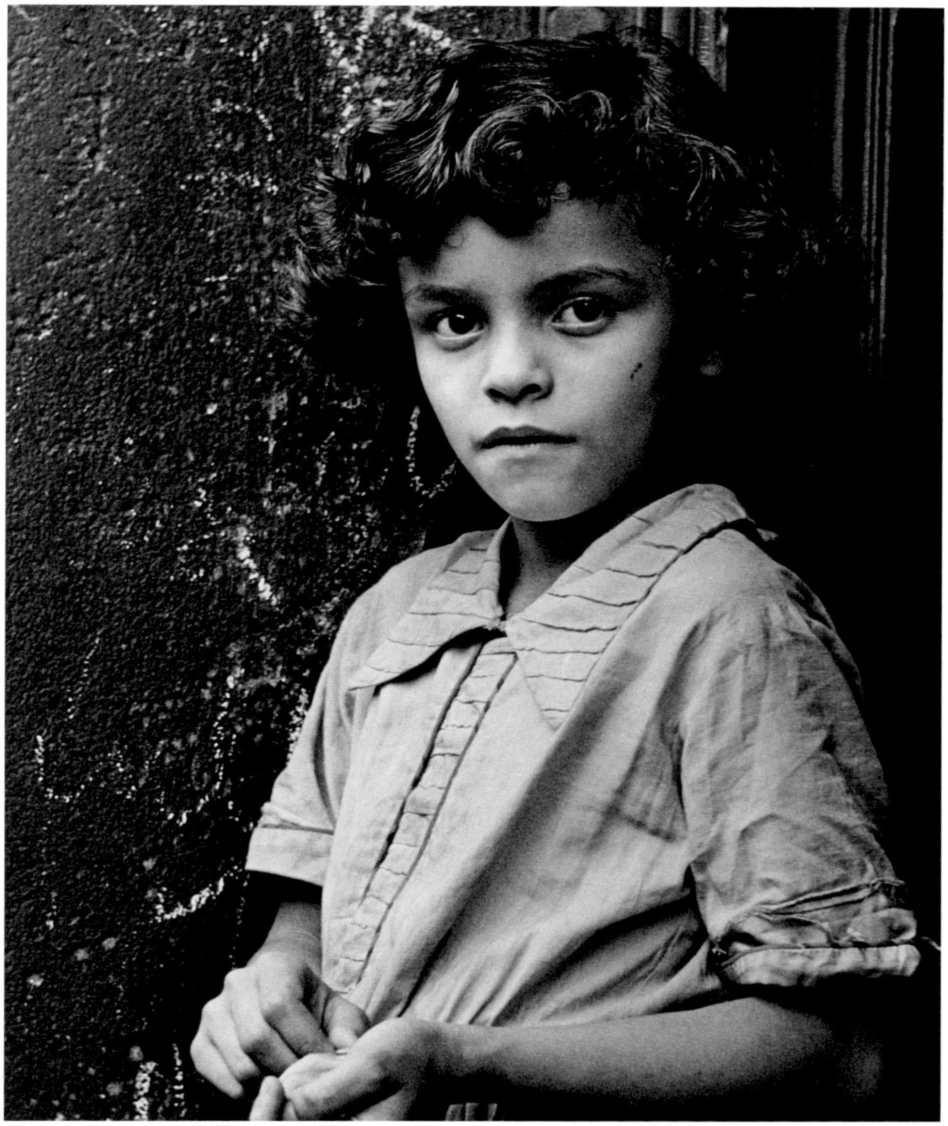

Portrait of a man, c. 1950

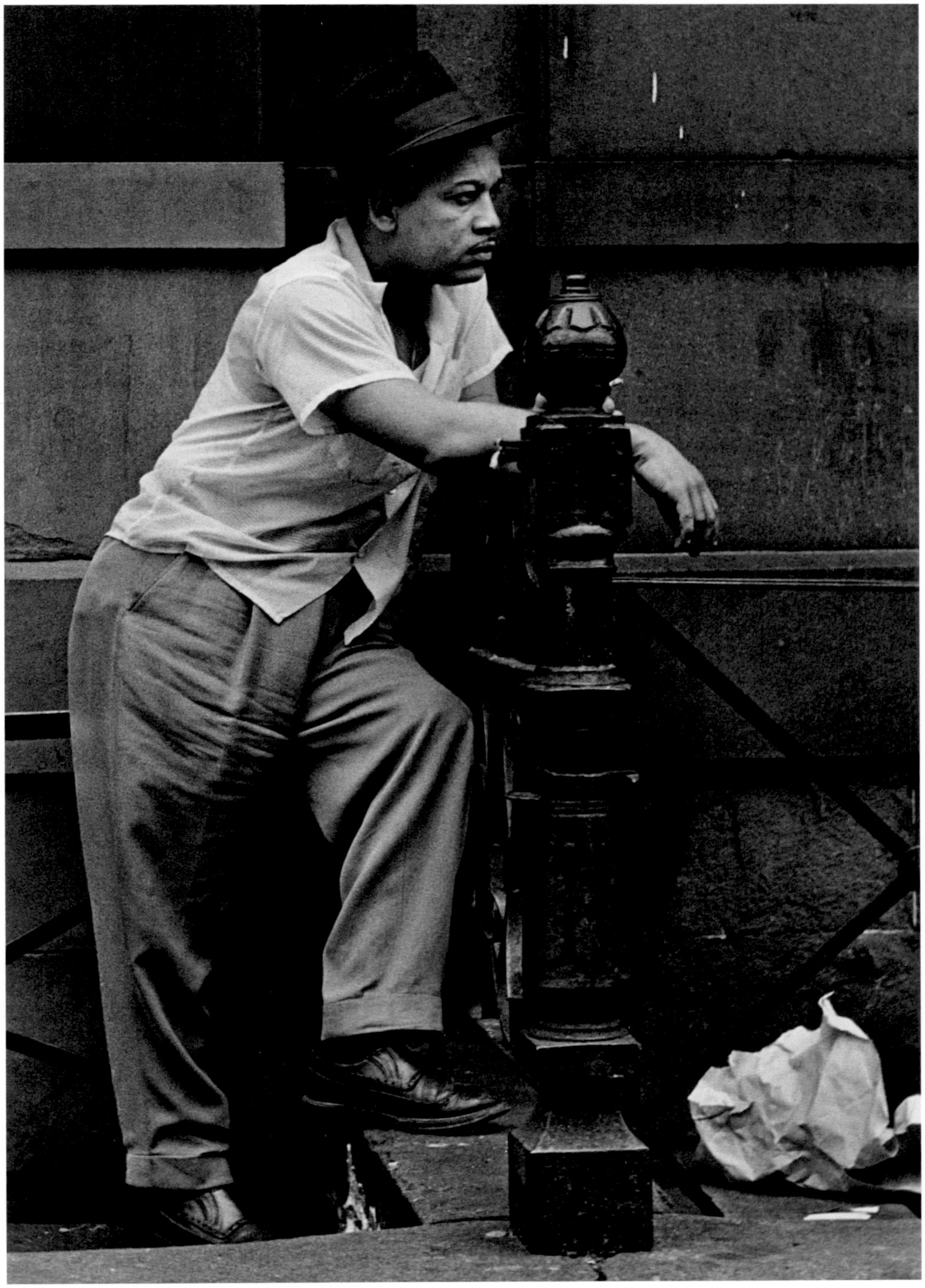

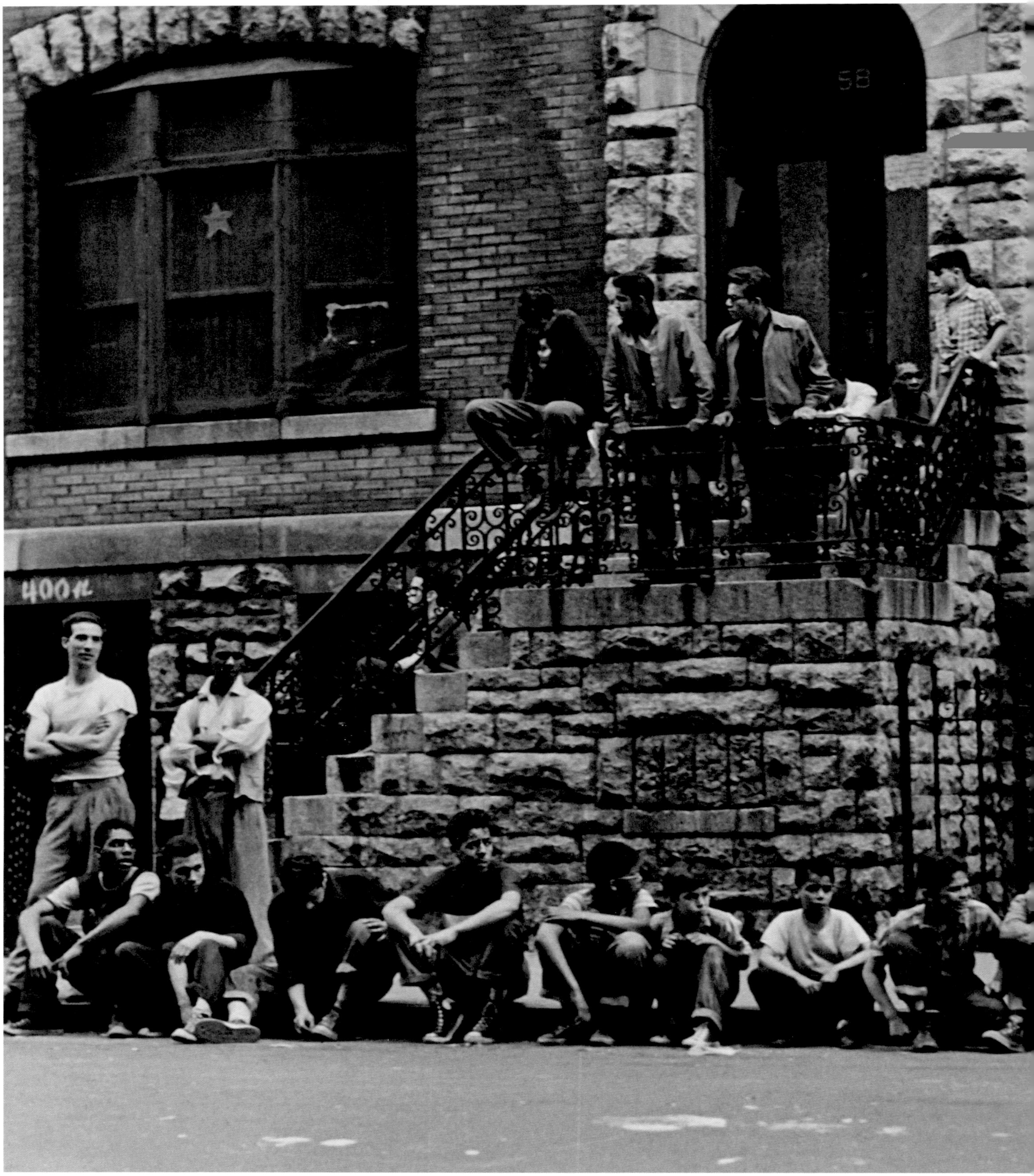
58

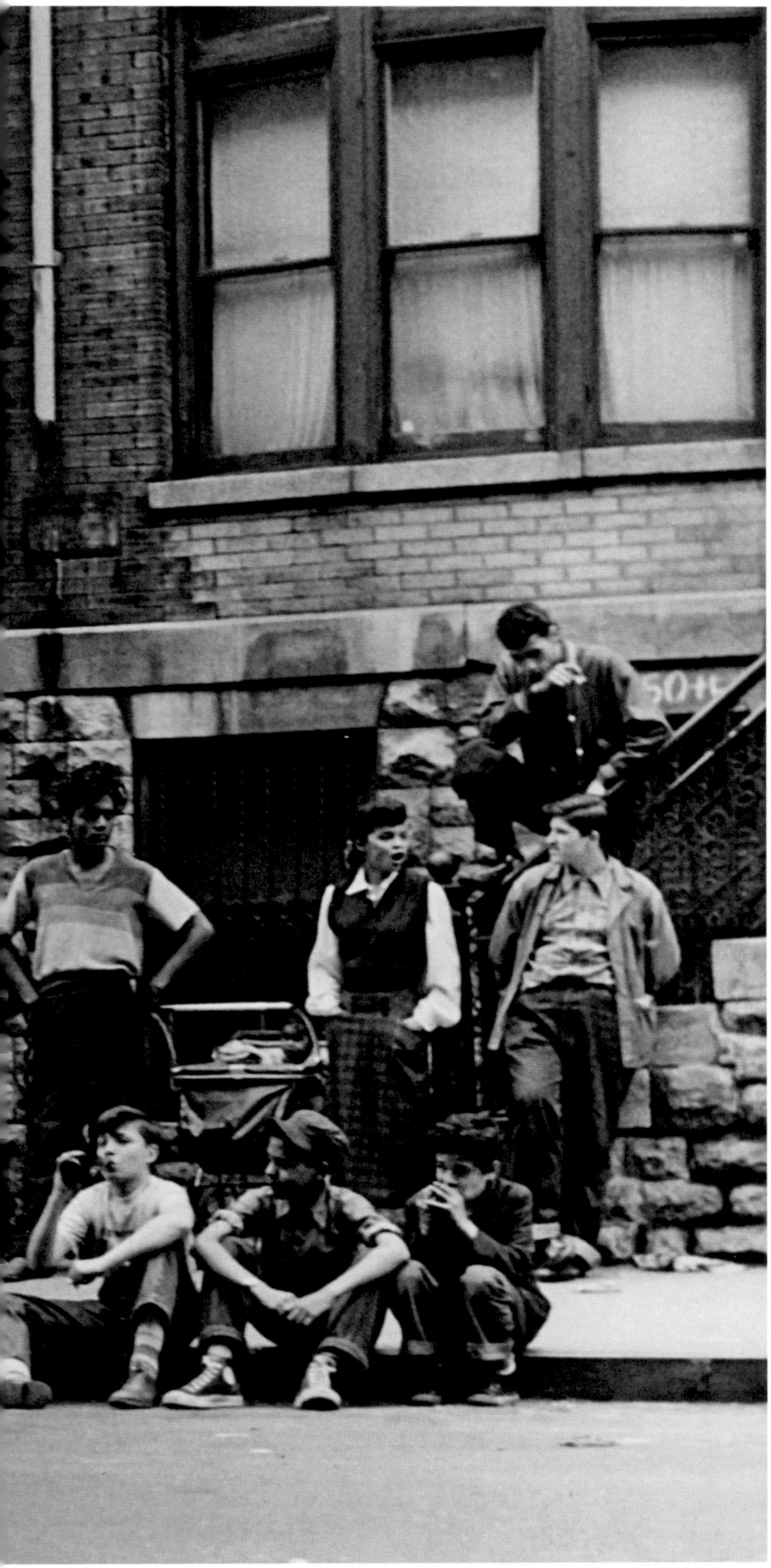

Watching a stickball game, c. 1950

76 No parking, c. 1950

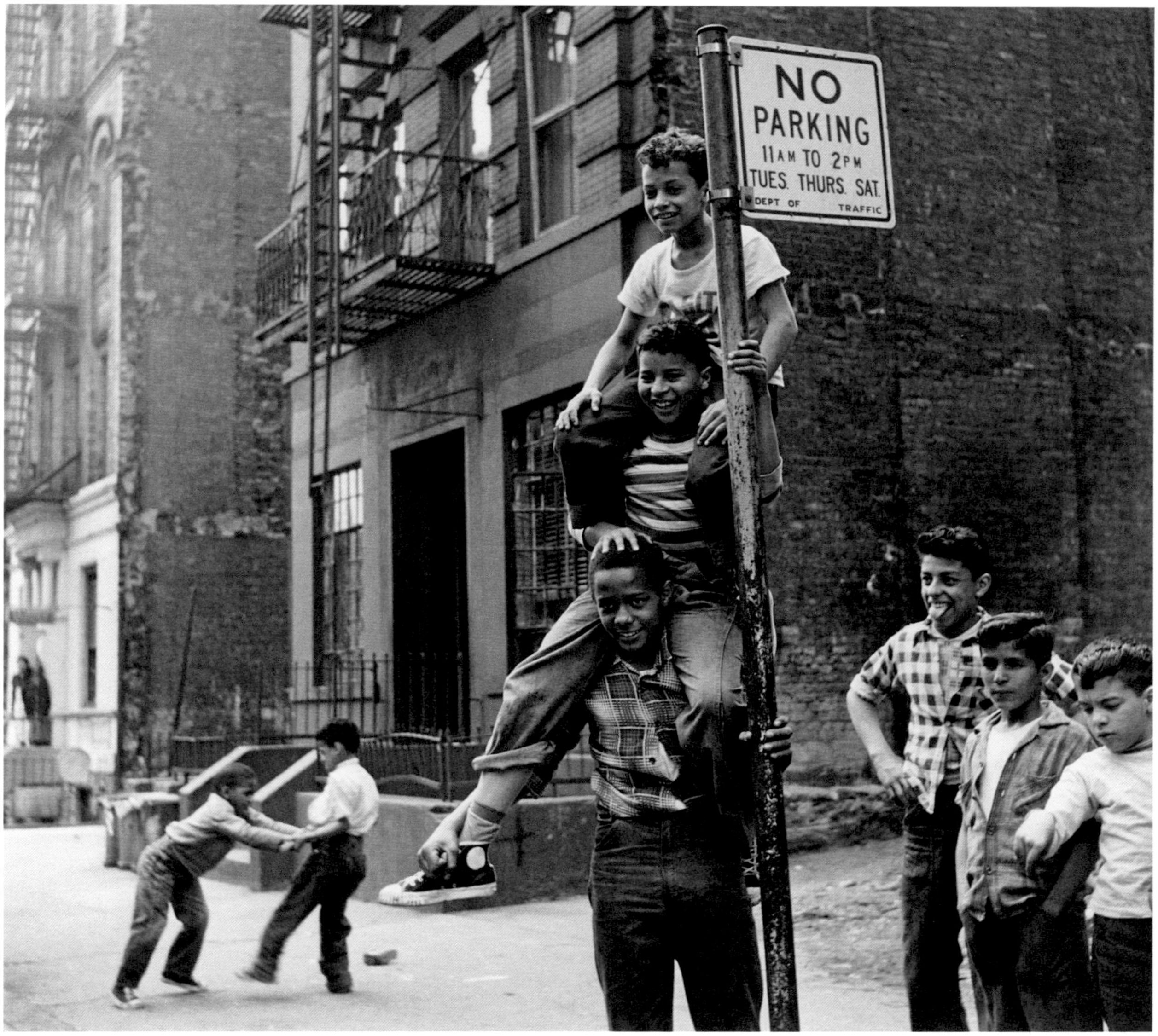
NO
PARKING
11AM TO 2PM
TUES. THURS. SAT.
DEPT OF TRAFFIC

Jumping for the basketball, c. 1950

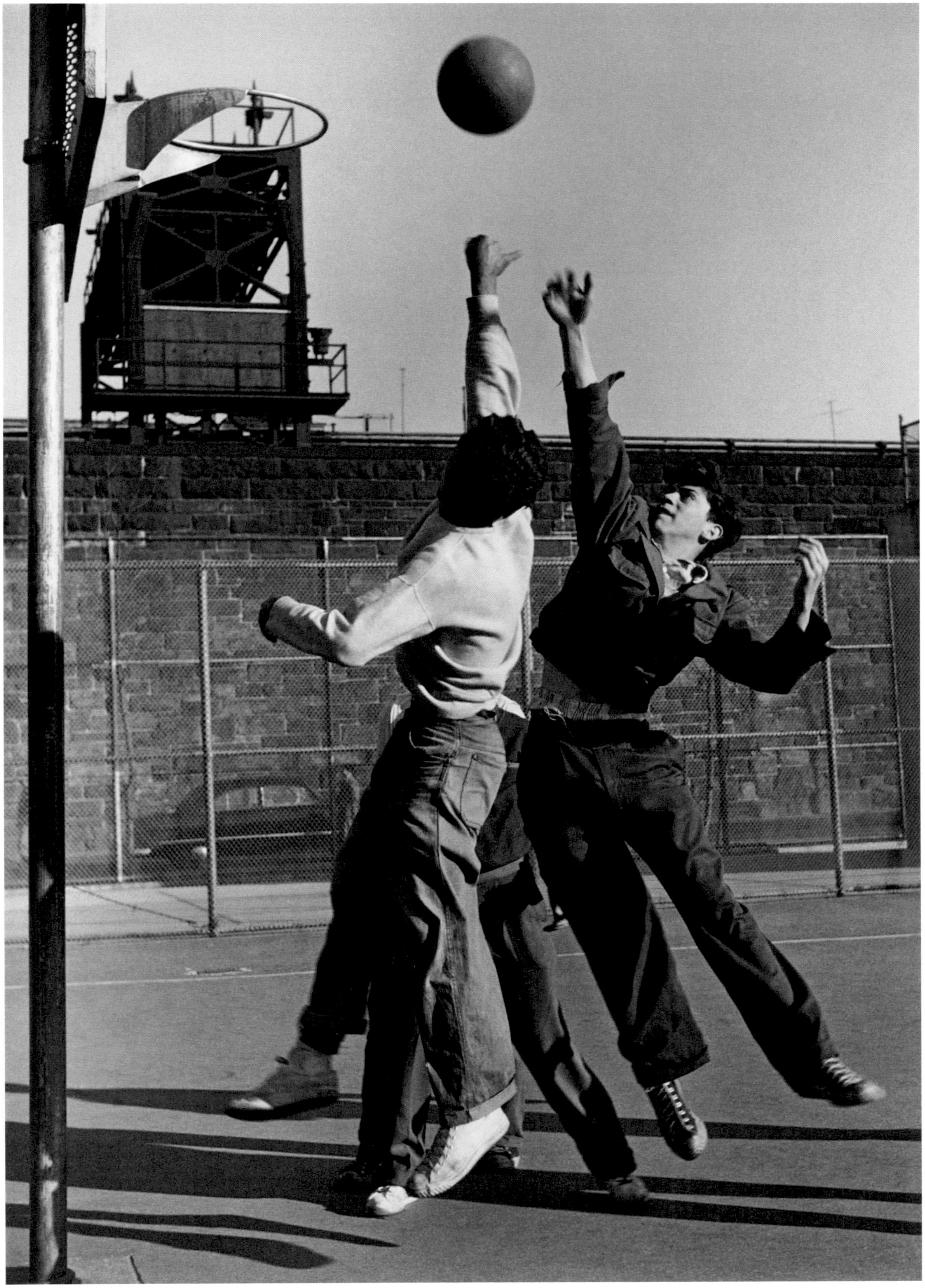

 Stickball players, c. 1950

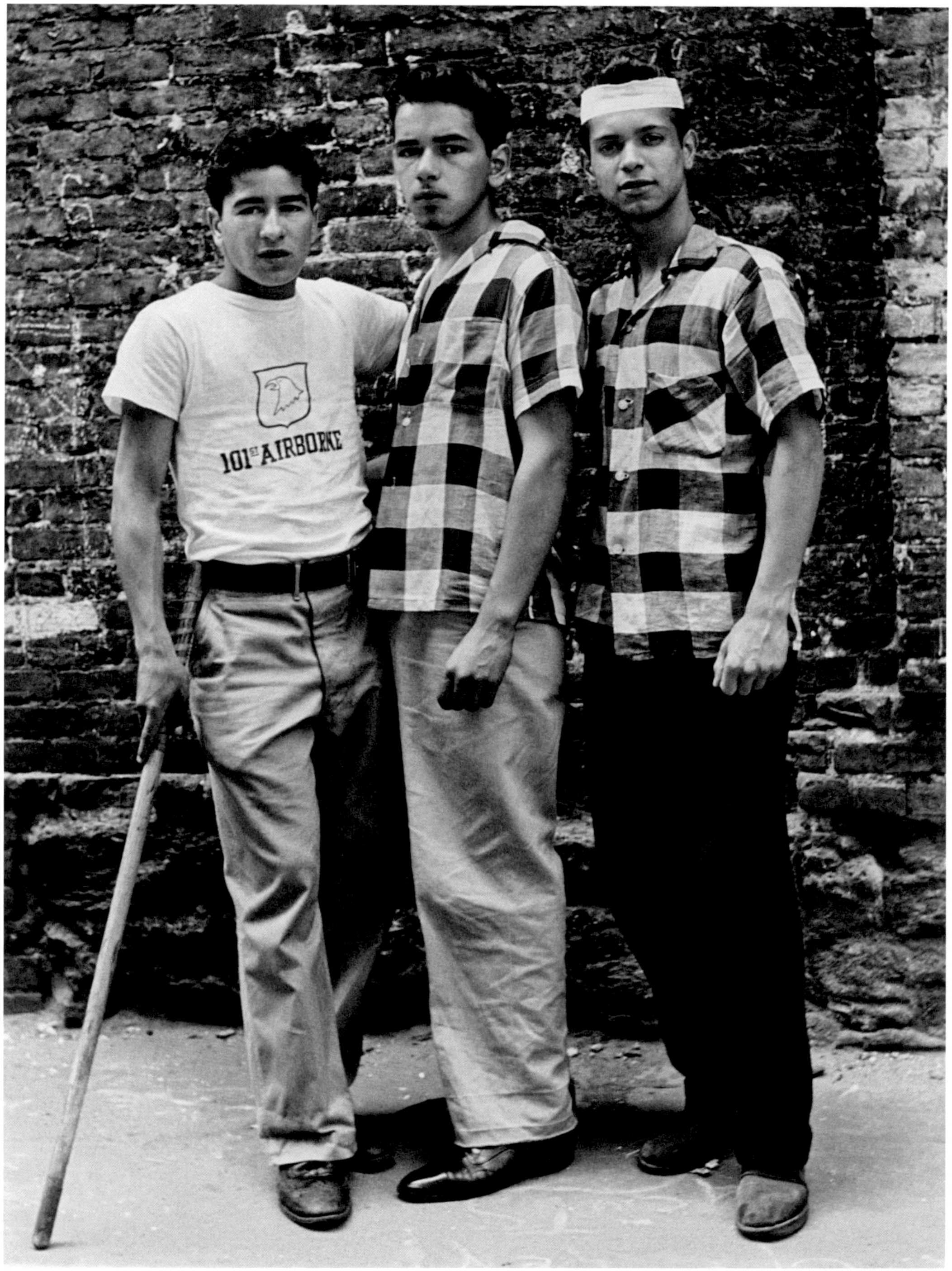
101ST AIRBORNE

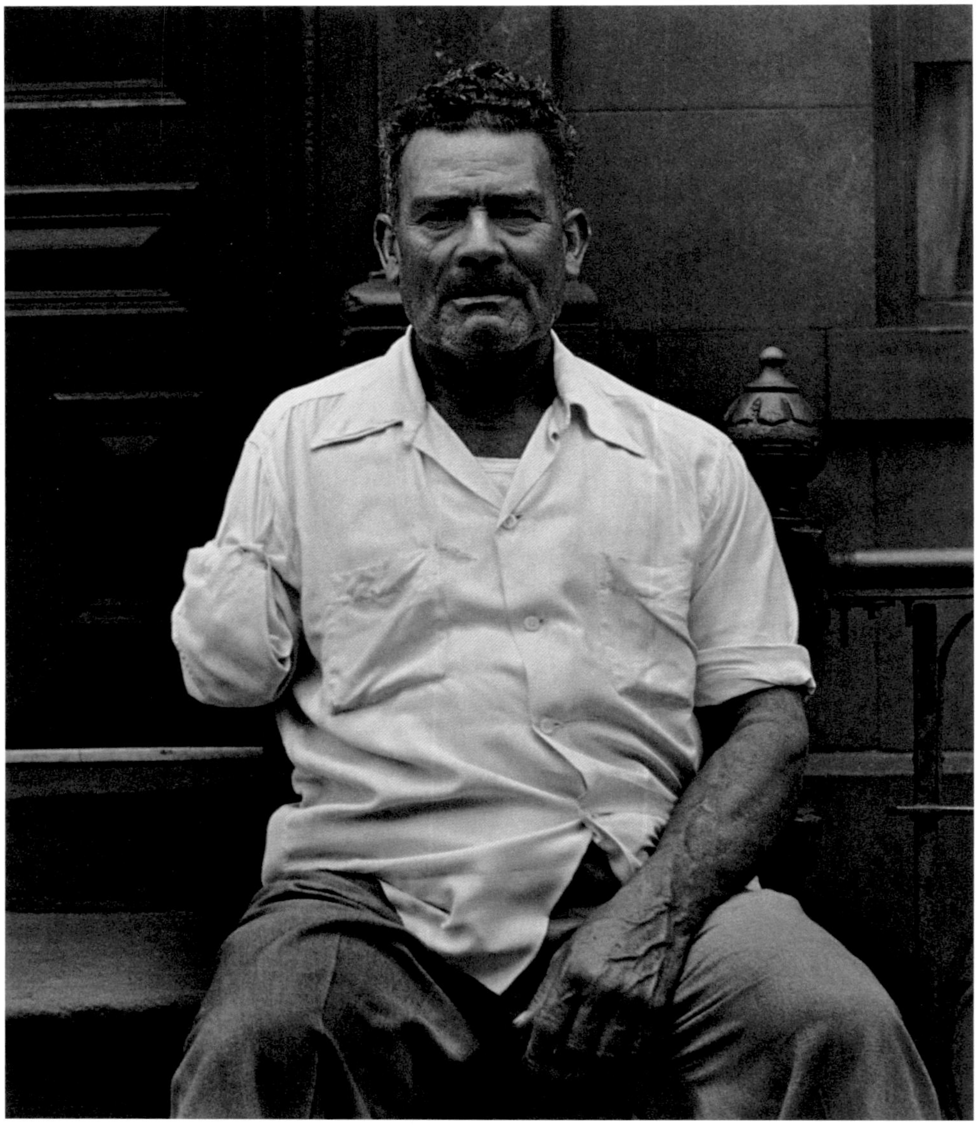

 Disabled worker, c. 1950

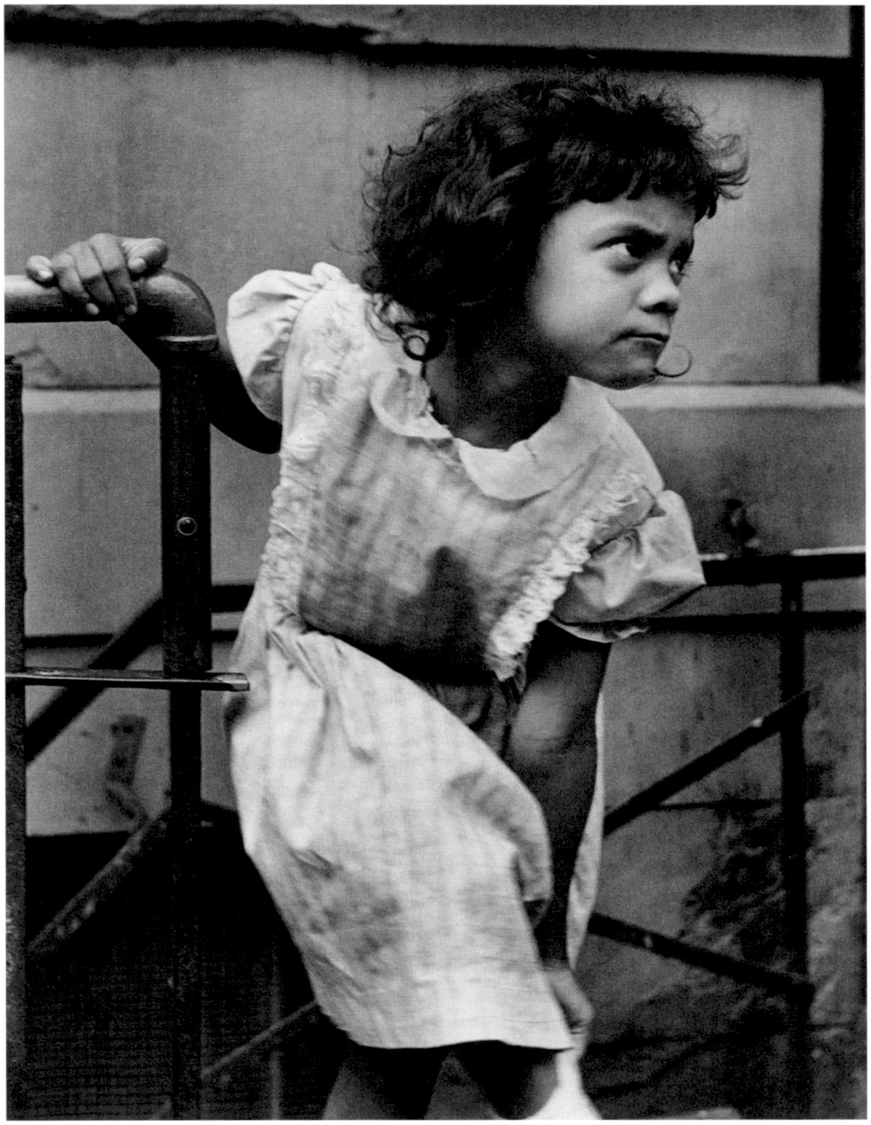

Girl pulling up her sock, c. 1950

84 Man and girl on stoop, c. 1950

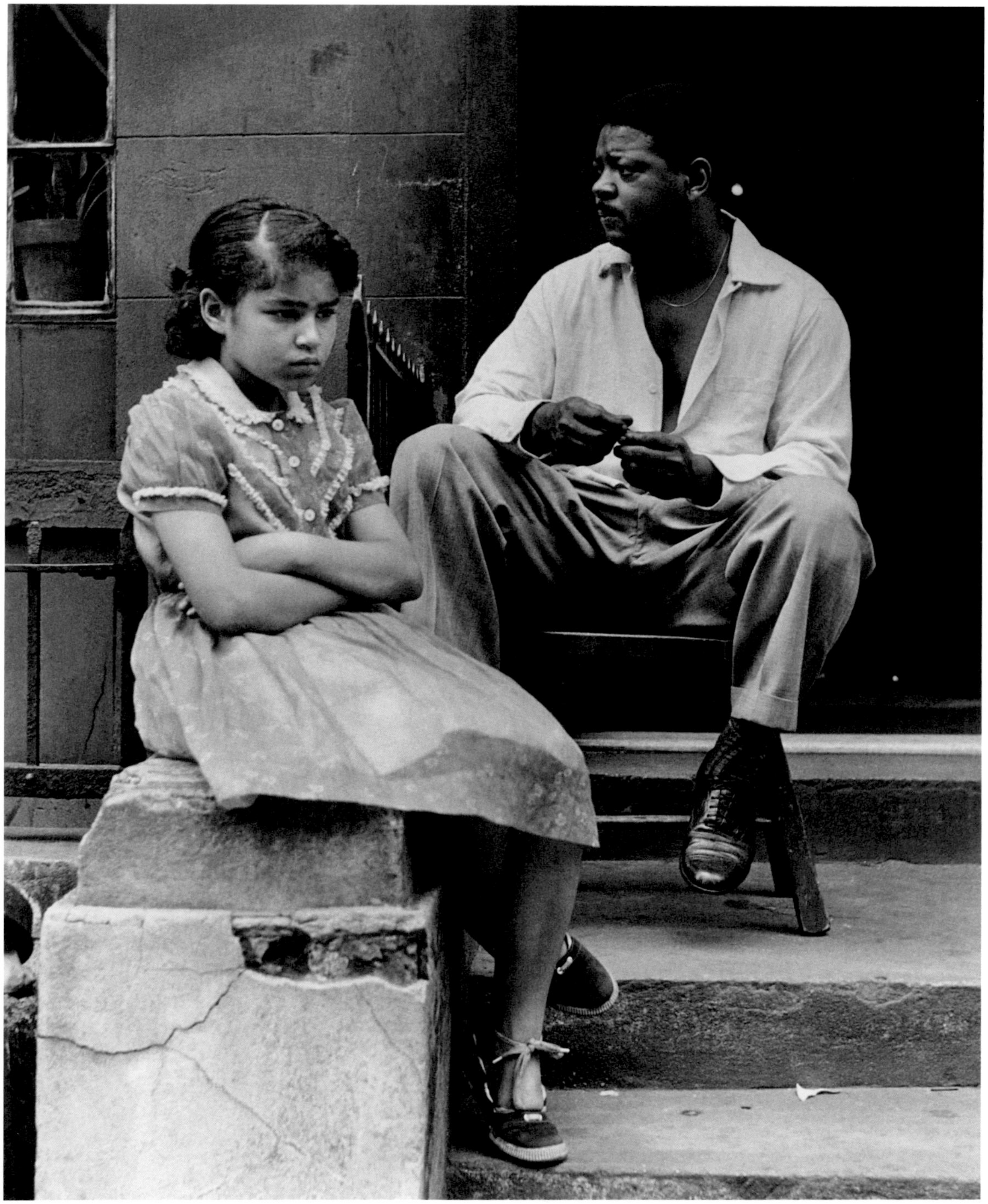

Grandfather and boy, c. 1950

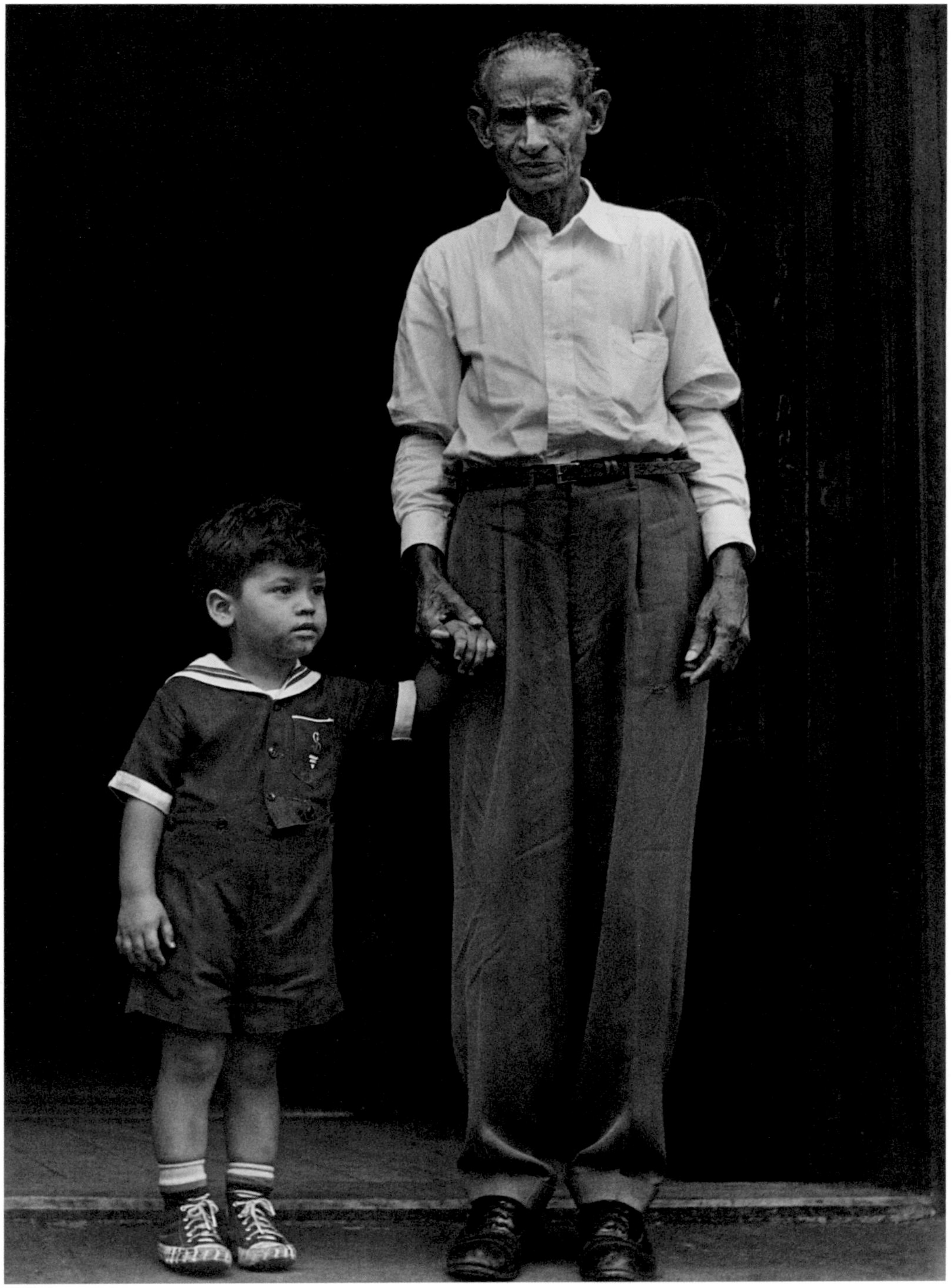

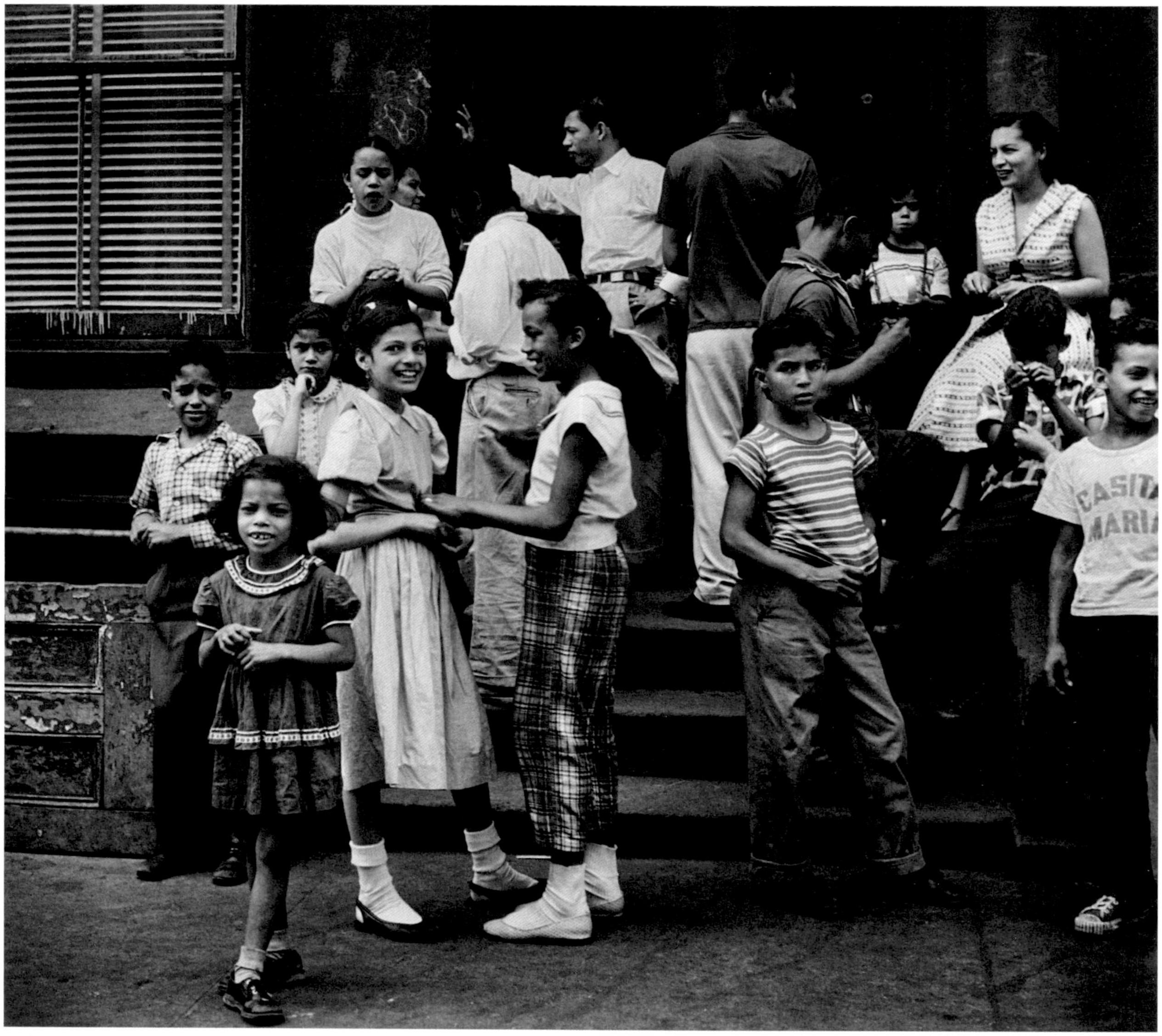
CASITA
MARIA

Children gathering at stoop, c. 1950

90 Elder hands, c. 1950

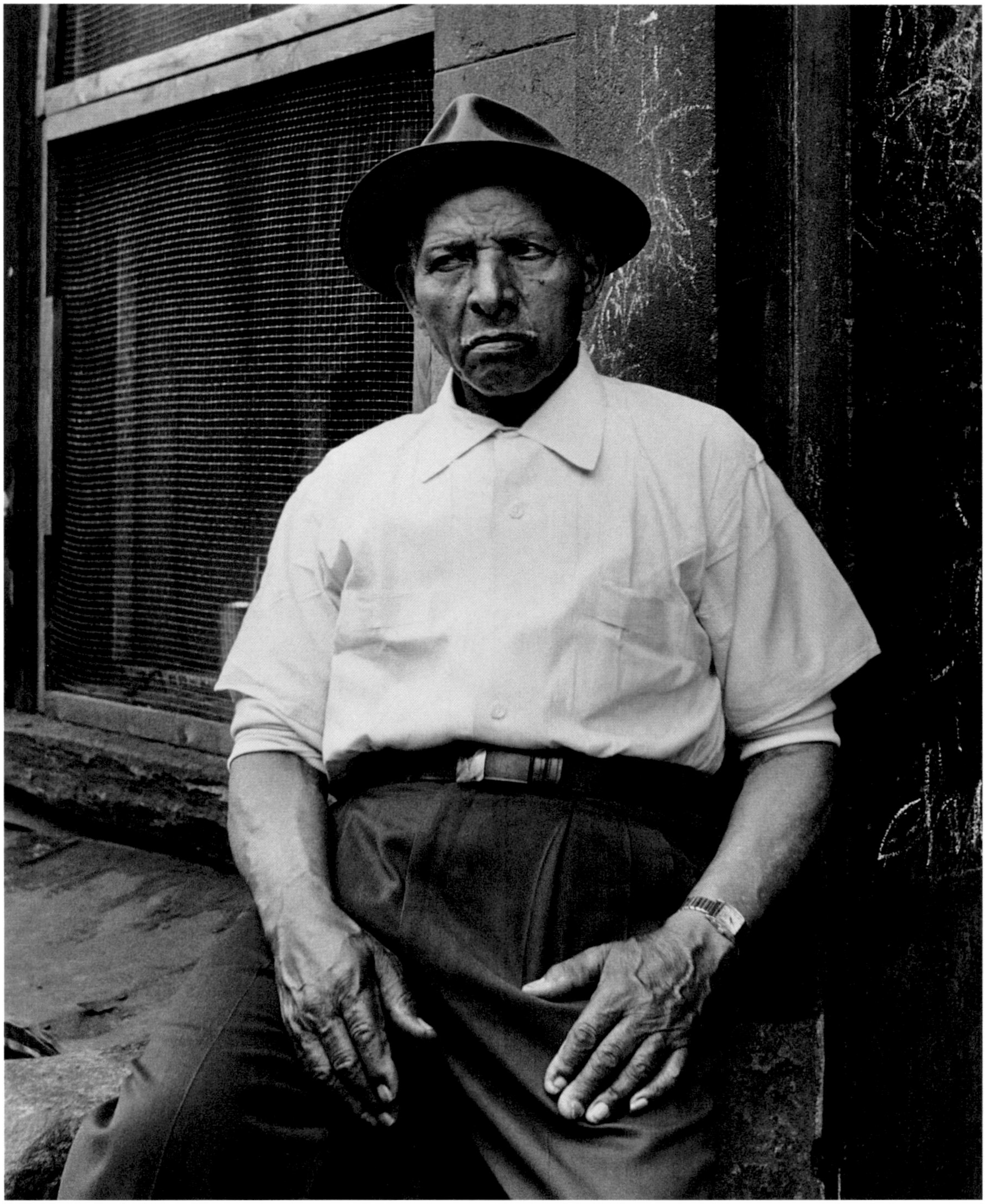

 Grandmother and child, c. 1950

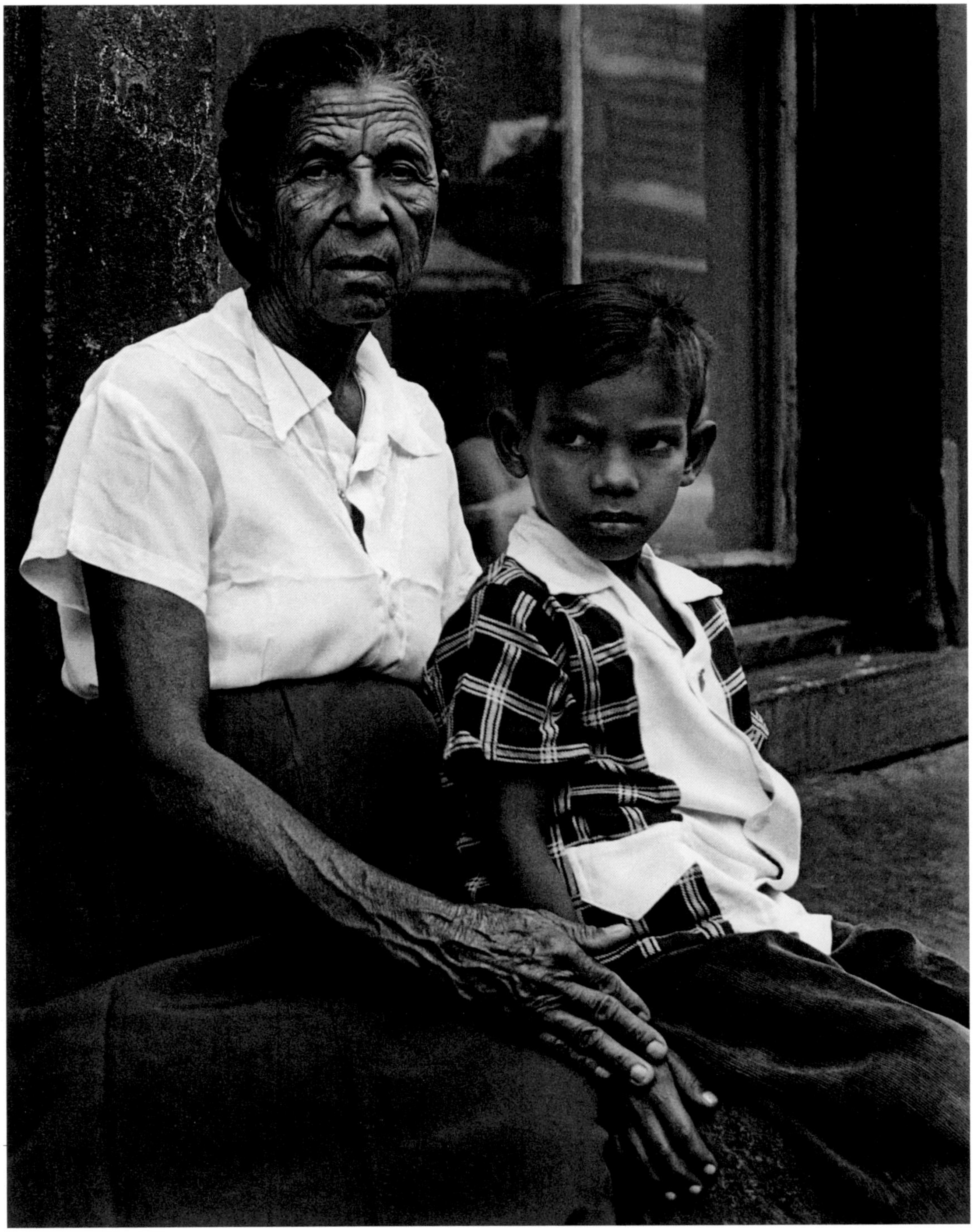

 Three young girls, c. 1950

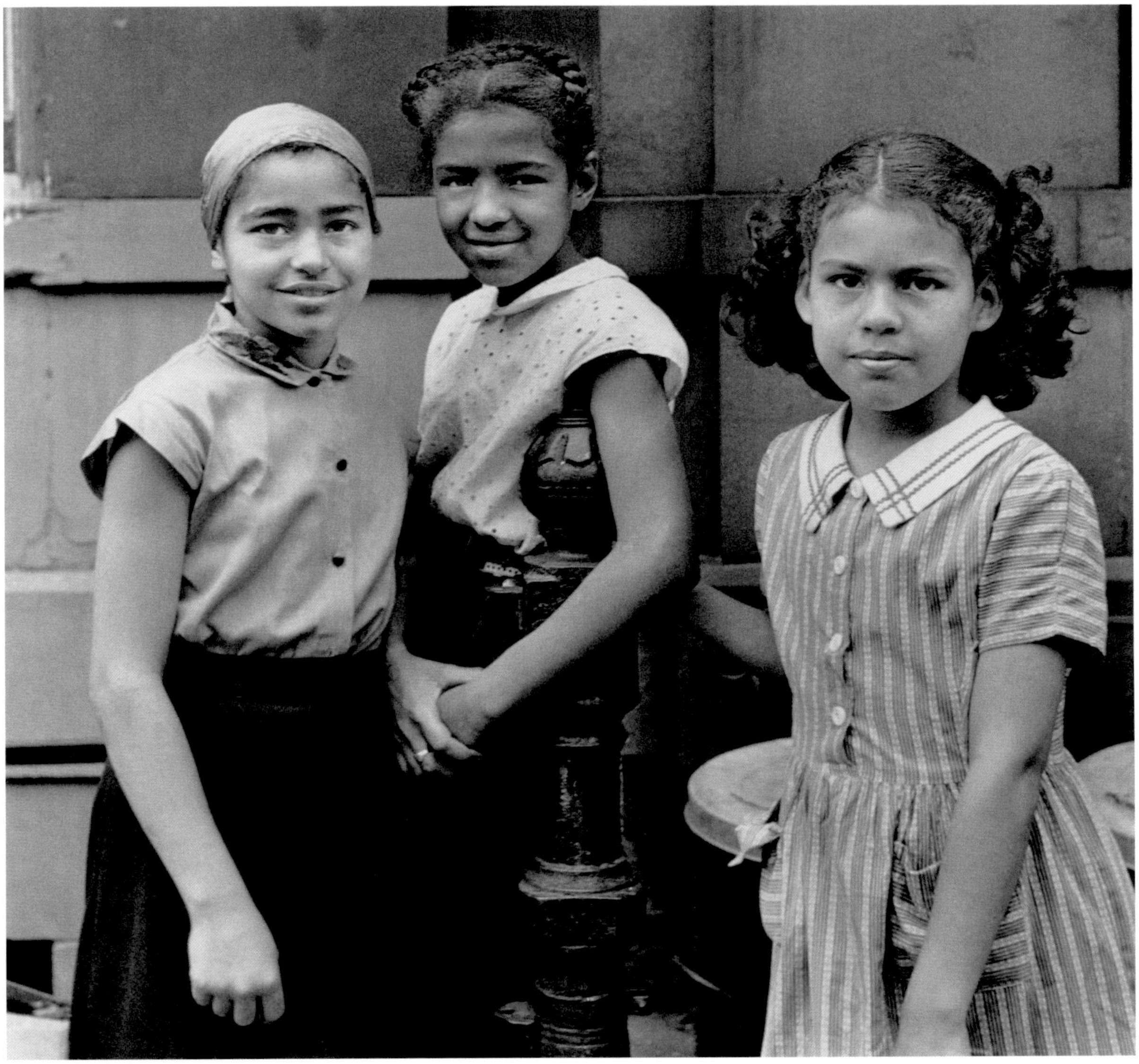

Boys playing ball, c. 1950

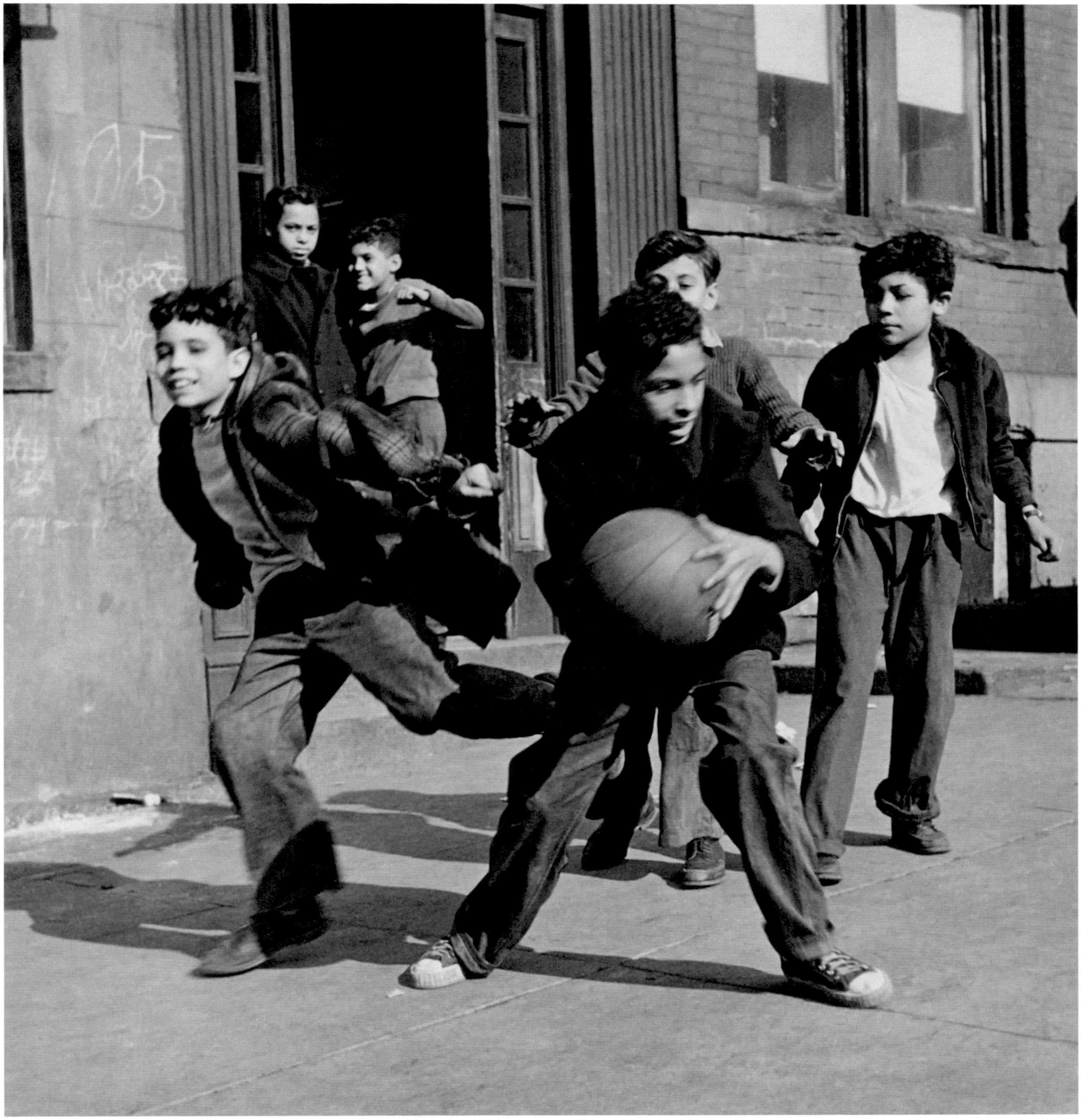

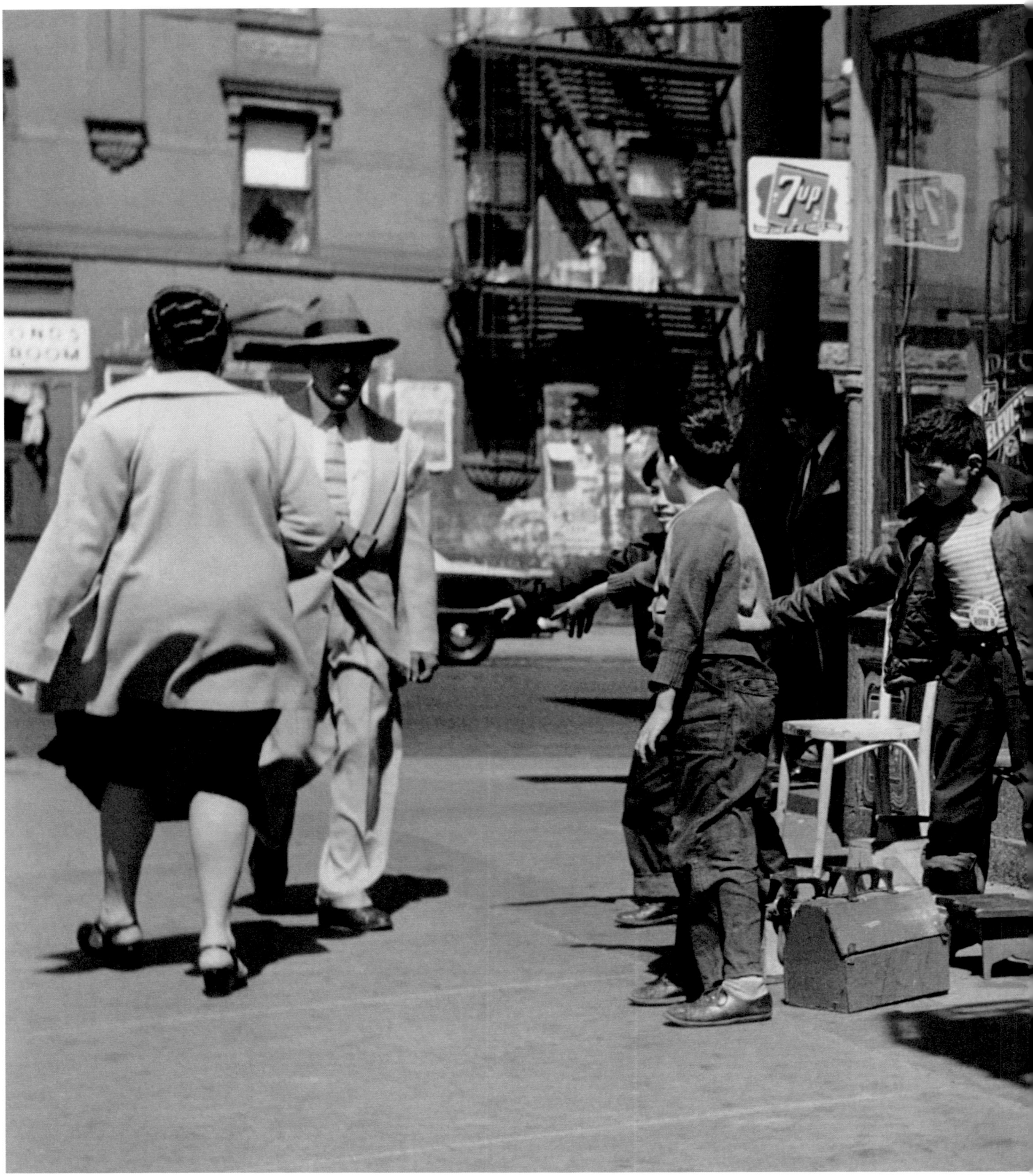
7up

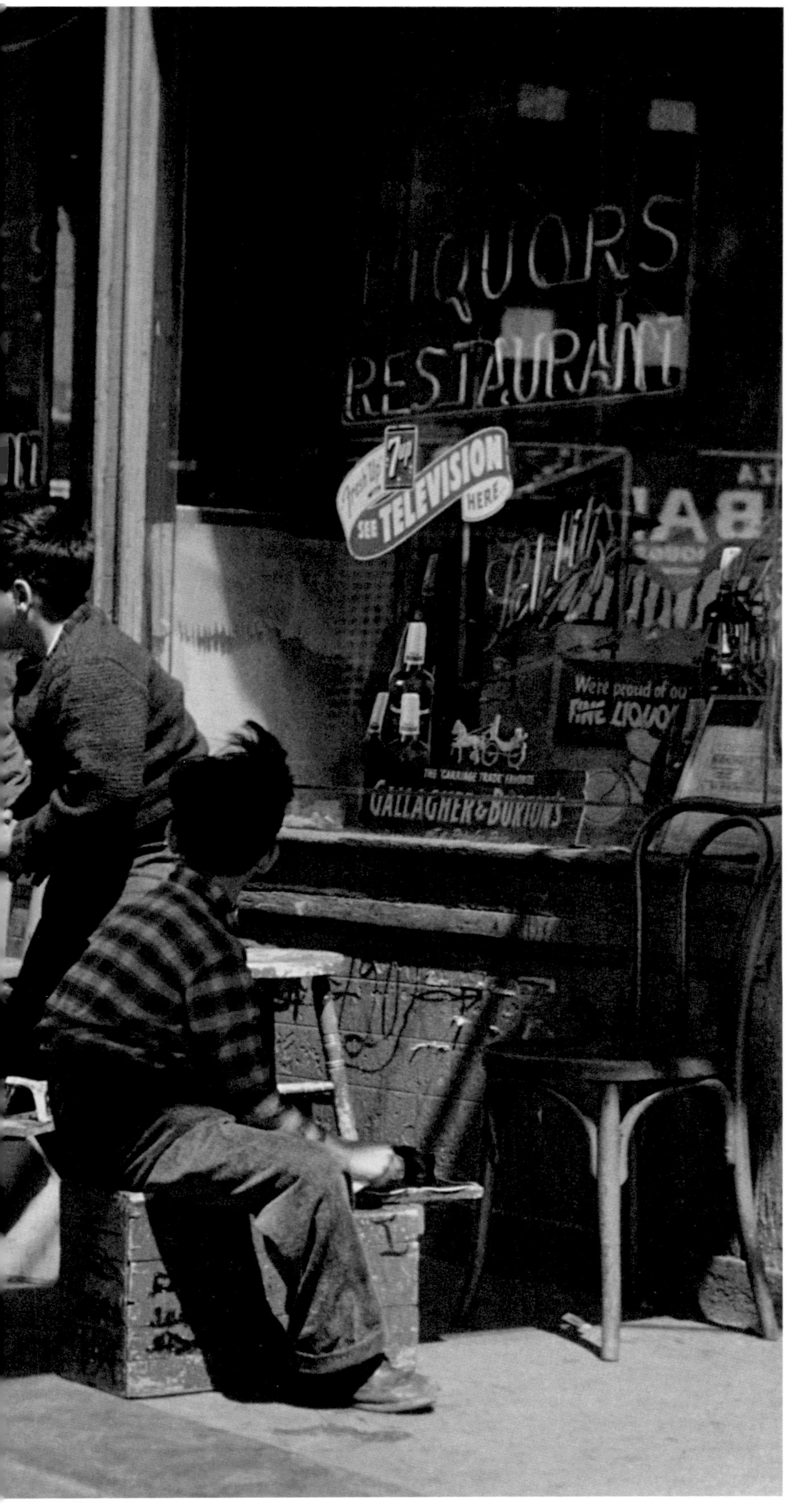

Shoeshine boys at work, East 110th Street, c. 1950

 Shoeshine boy with box, c. 1950

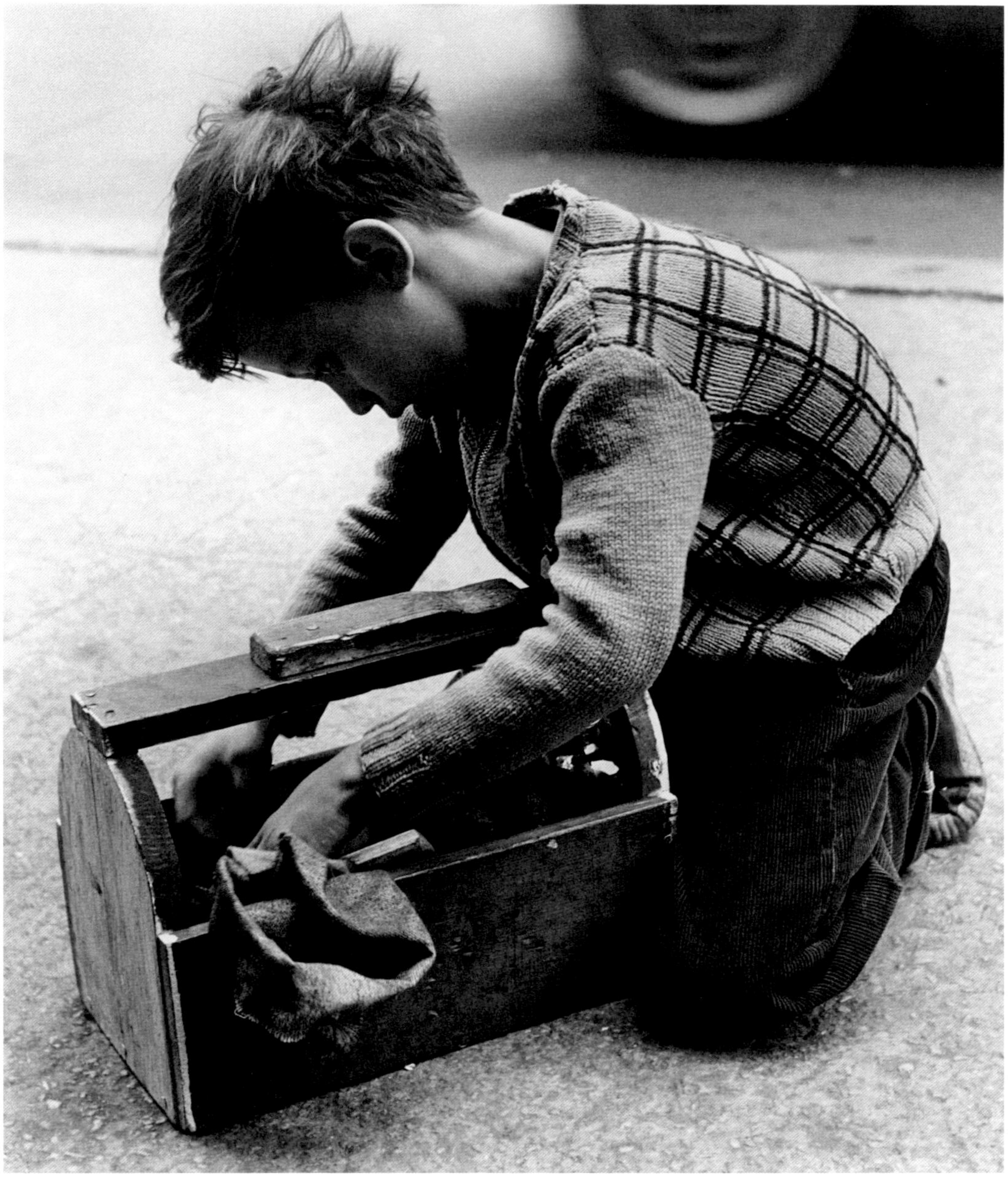

Boys playing on cart, 1951

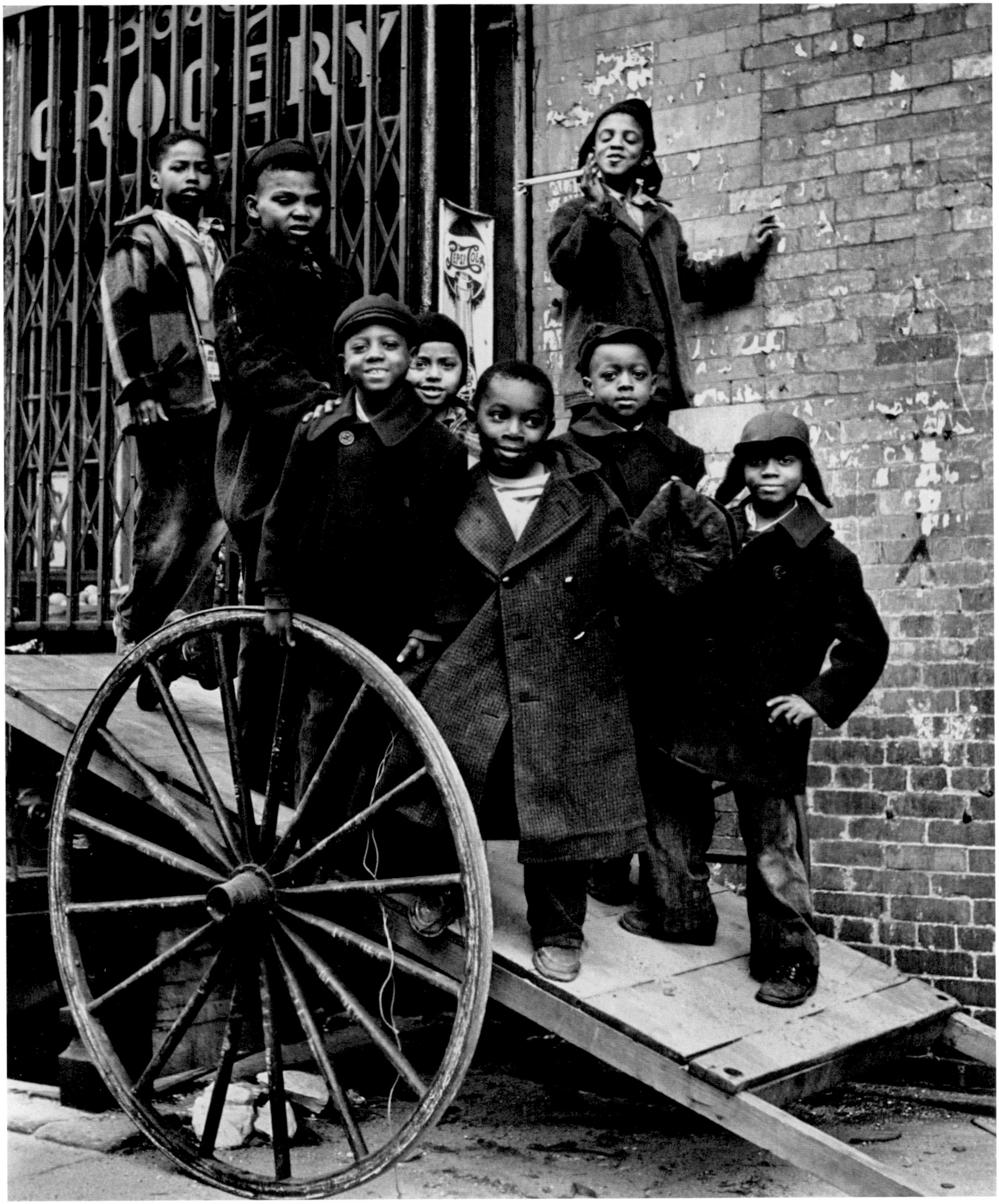
GROCERY
Pepsi-Cola

Boy, East 110th Street, 1951

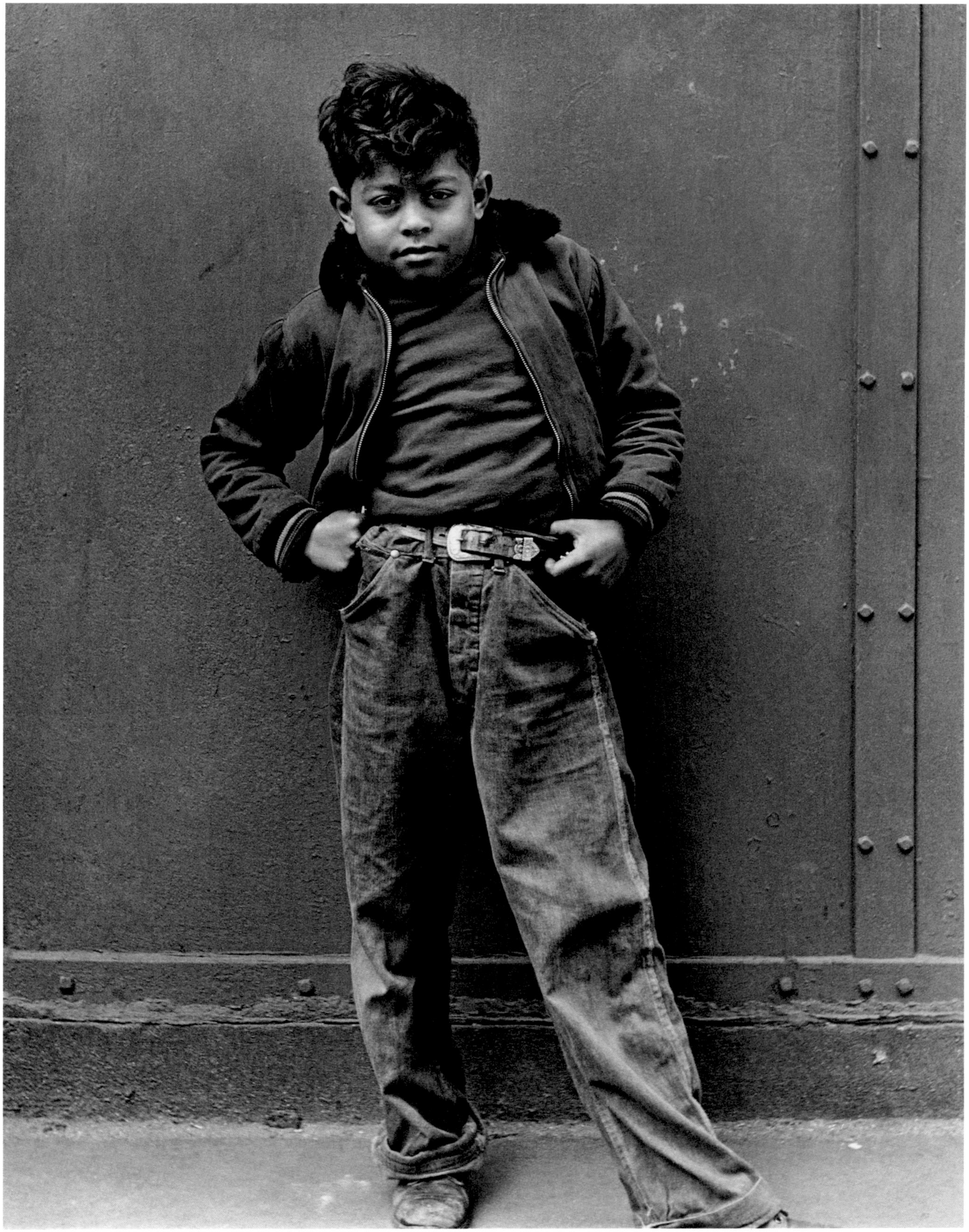

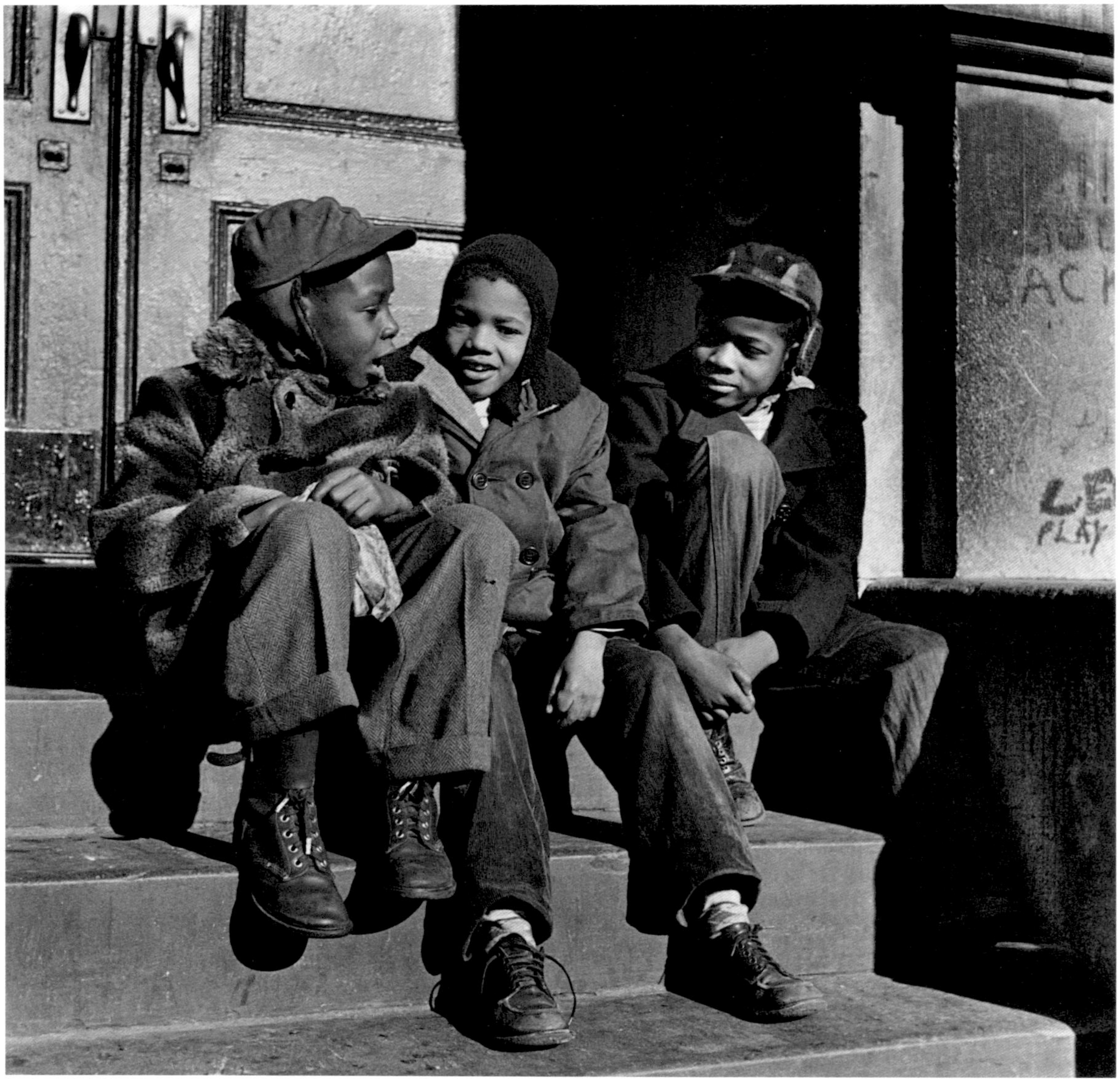
PLAY

Sunday best, c. 1950

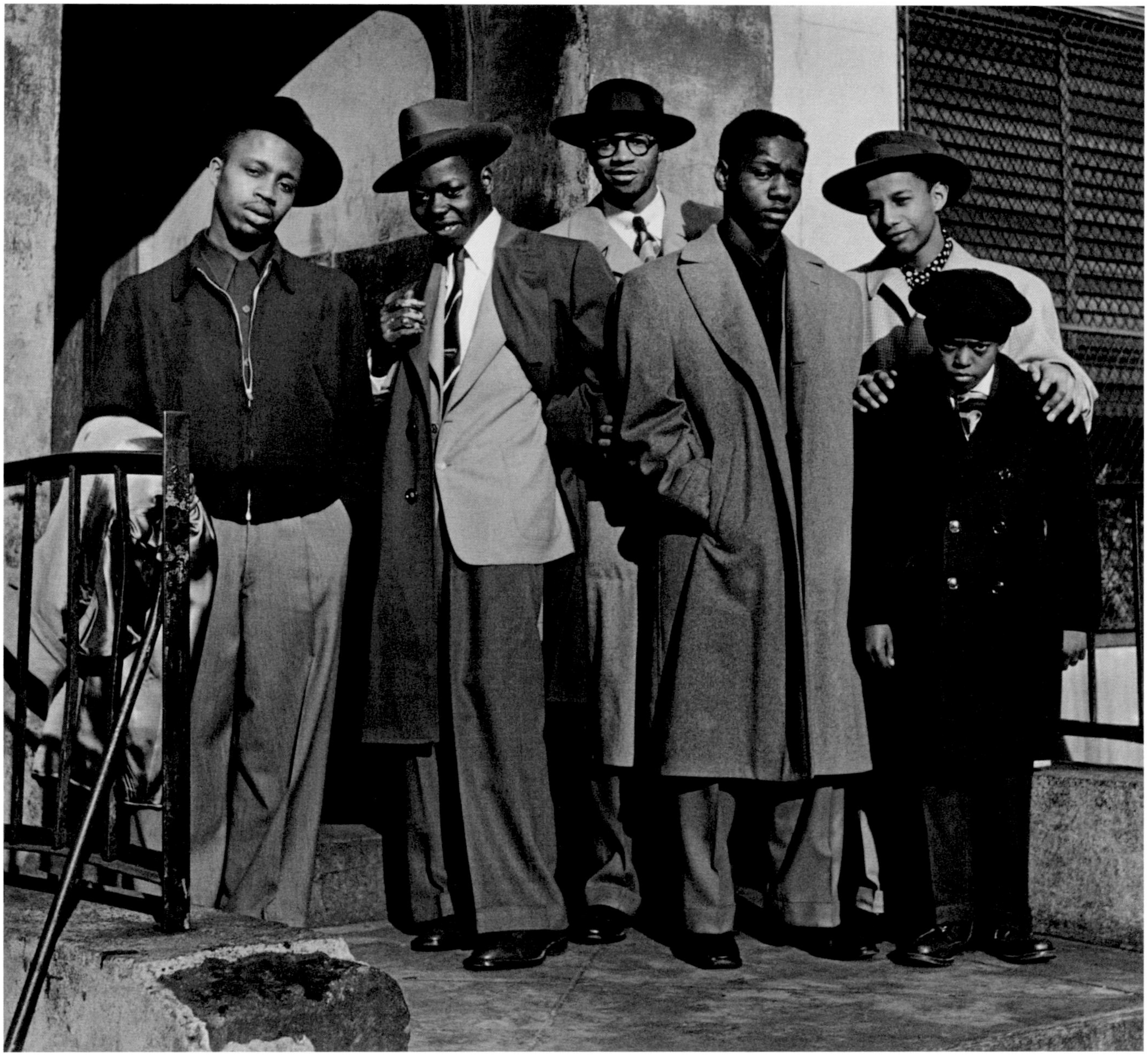

Street photographer, c. 1950

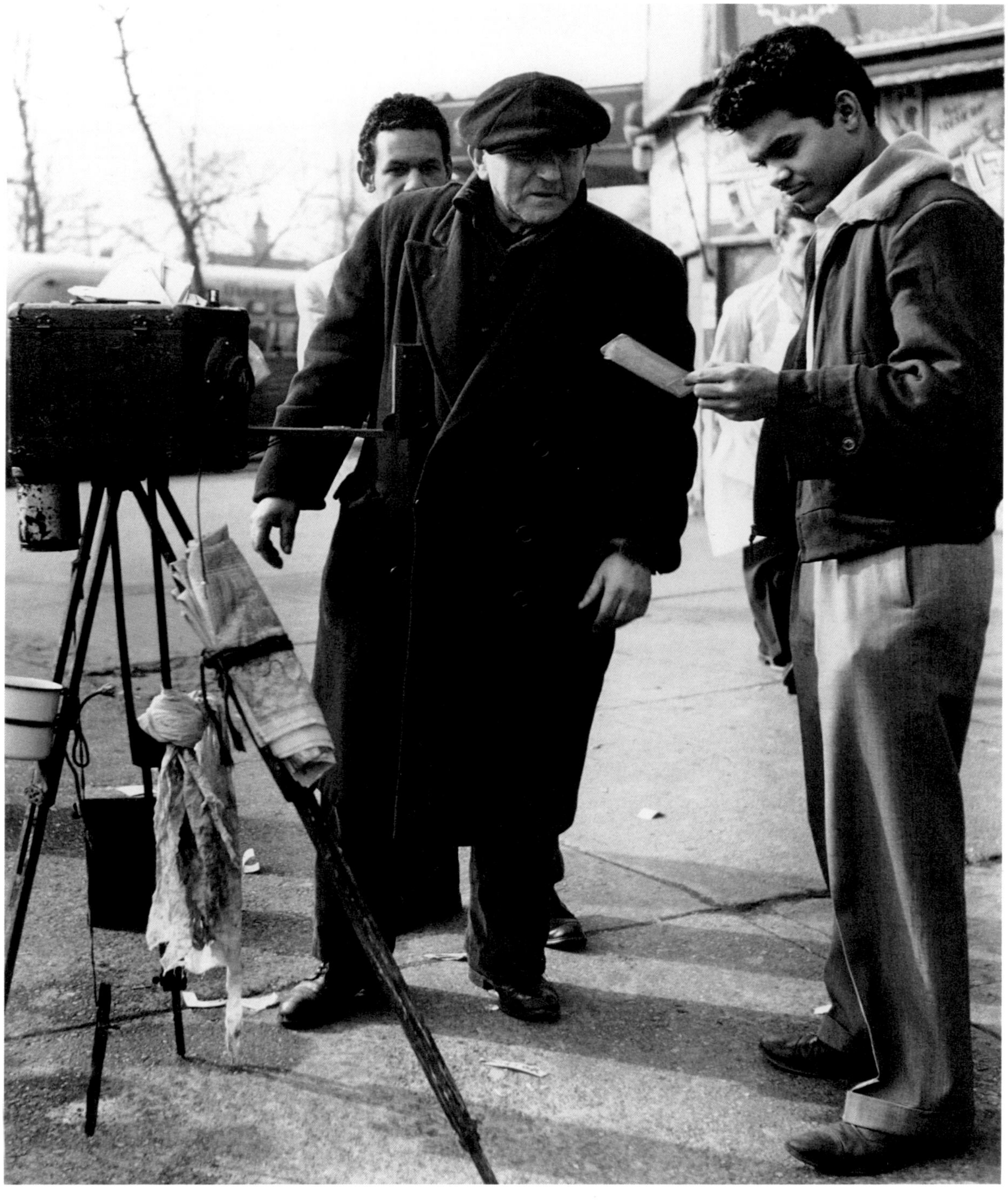

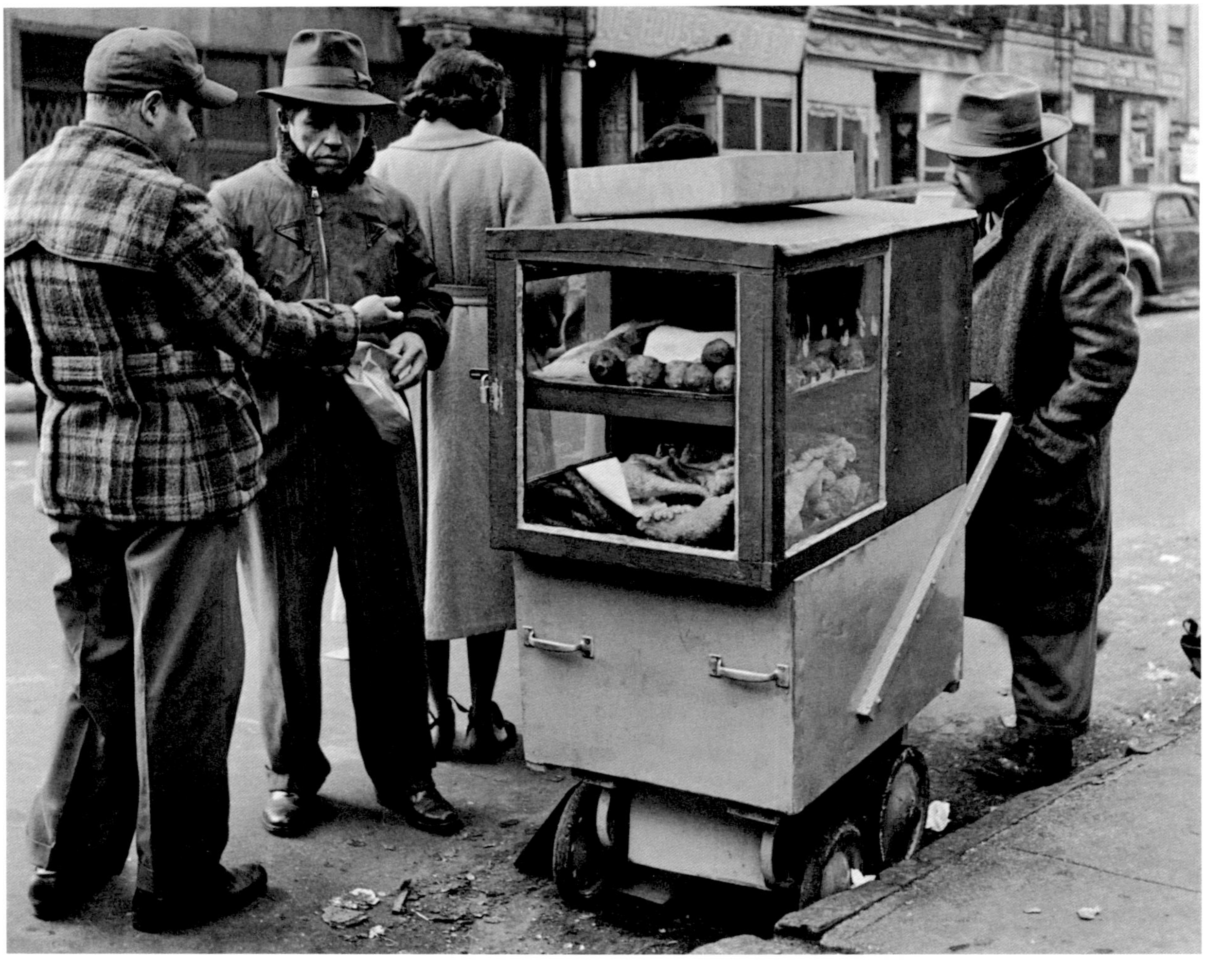

Cuchifrito vendor, East 100th Street, c. 1950

Public Market, Shopping bag vendor, East 110th Street, 1951

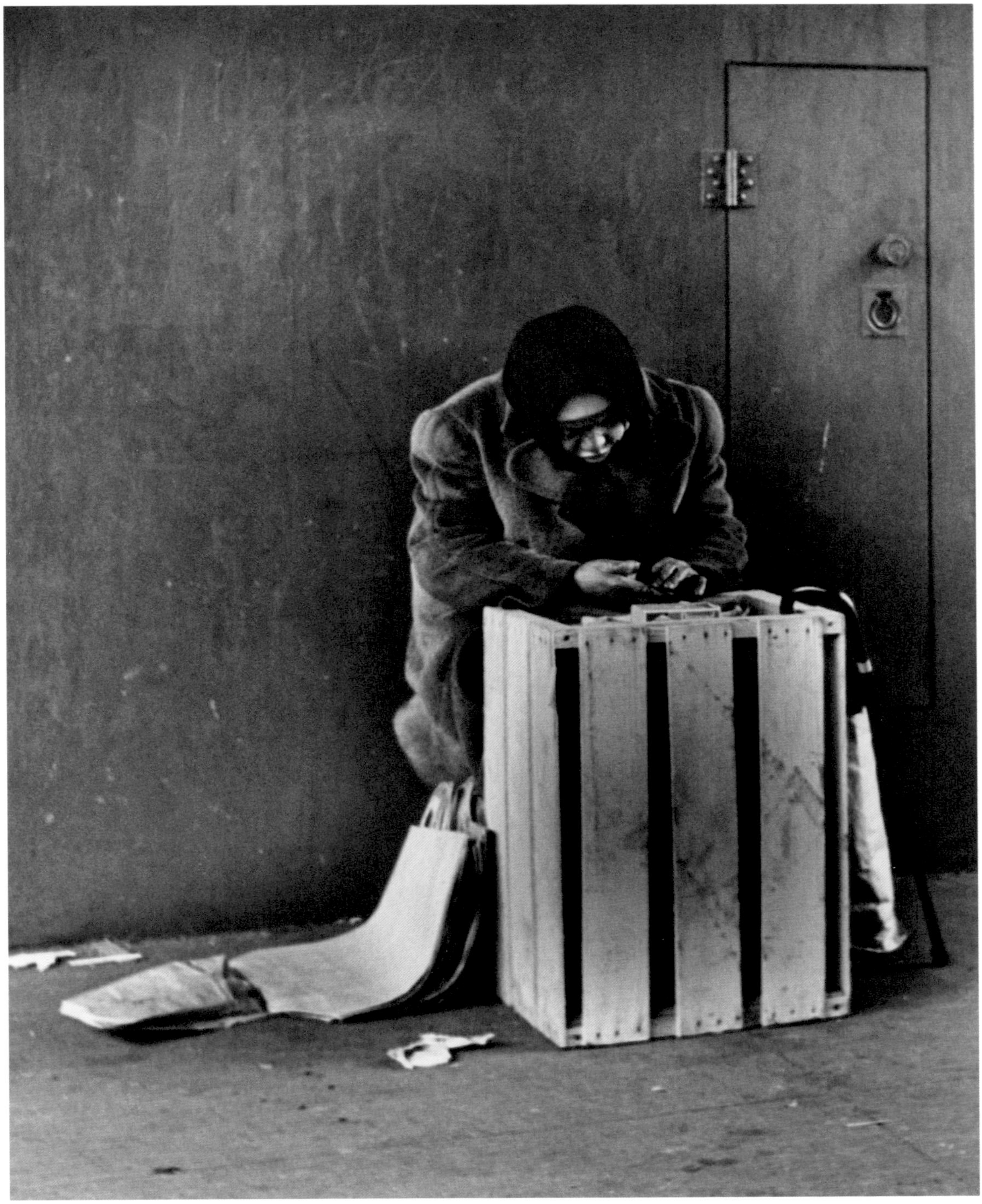

Shoeshine boy with chair, c. 1950

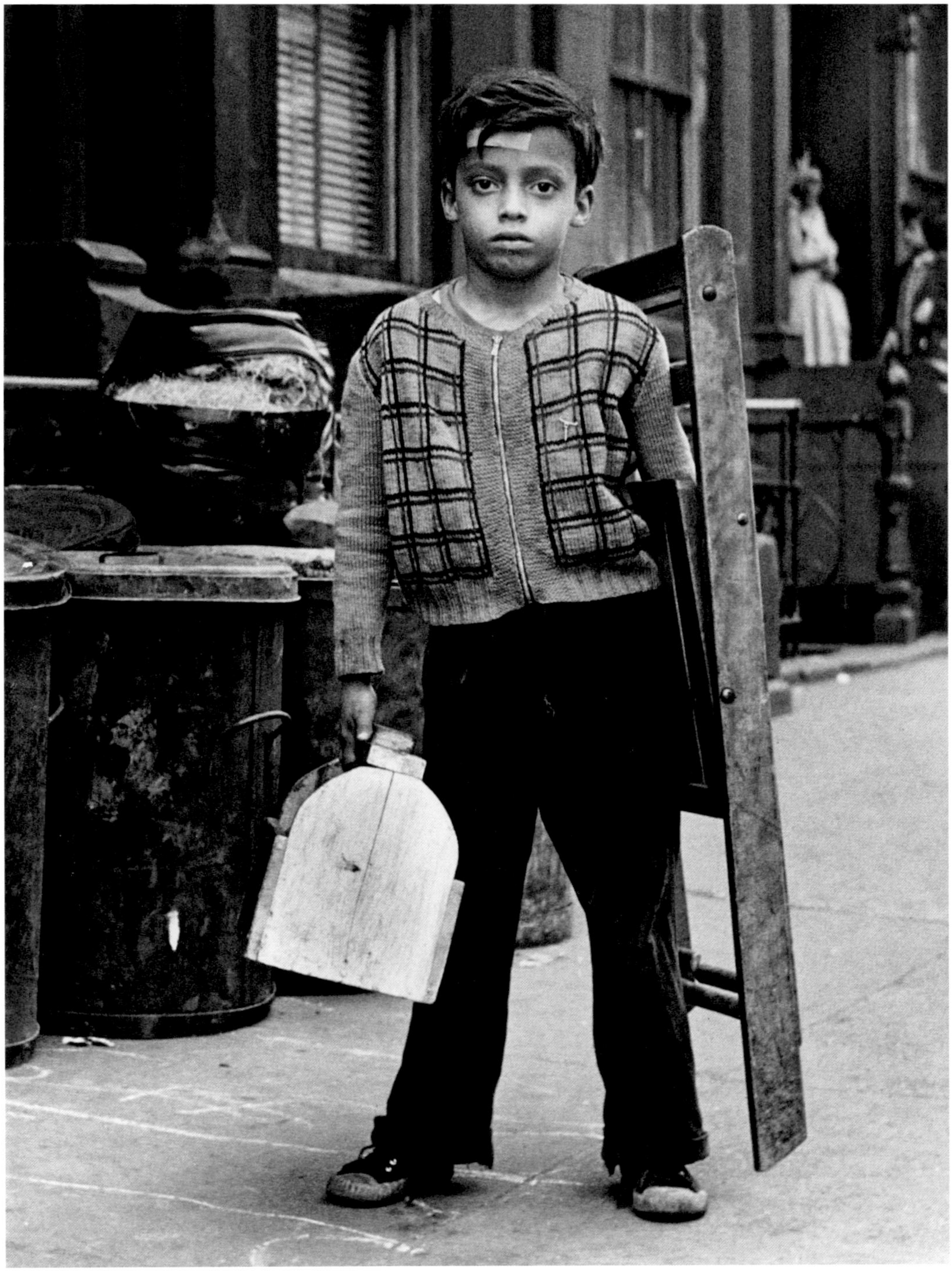

 Sleeping sisters, c. 1950

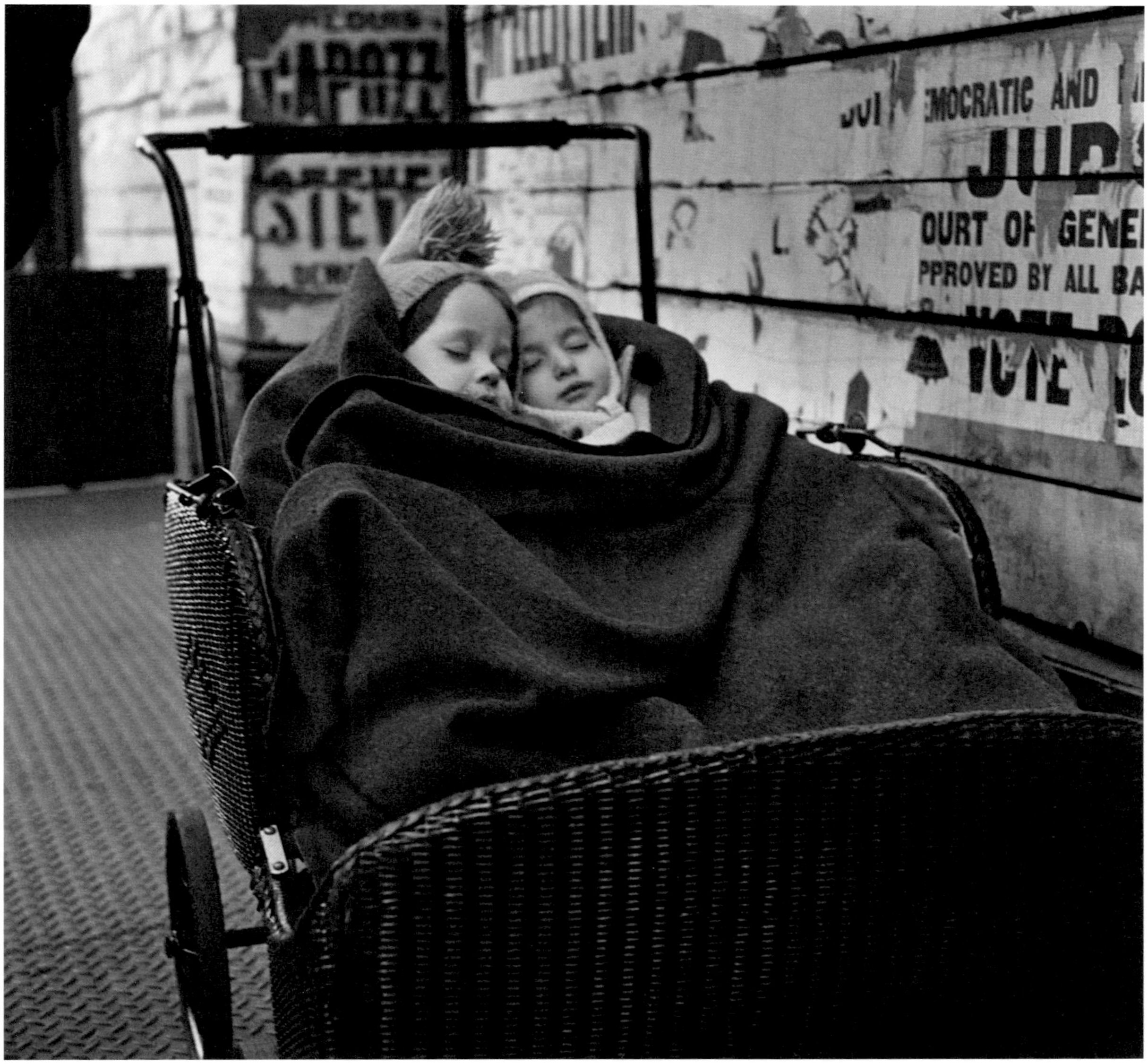
EMOCRATIC AND
OURT OF GENE
PPROVED BY ALL BA

Portrait of a girl, c. 1949

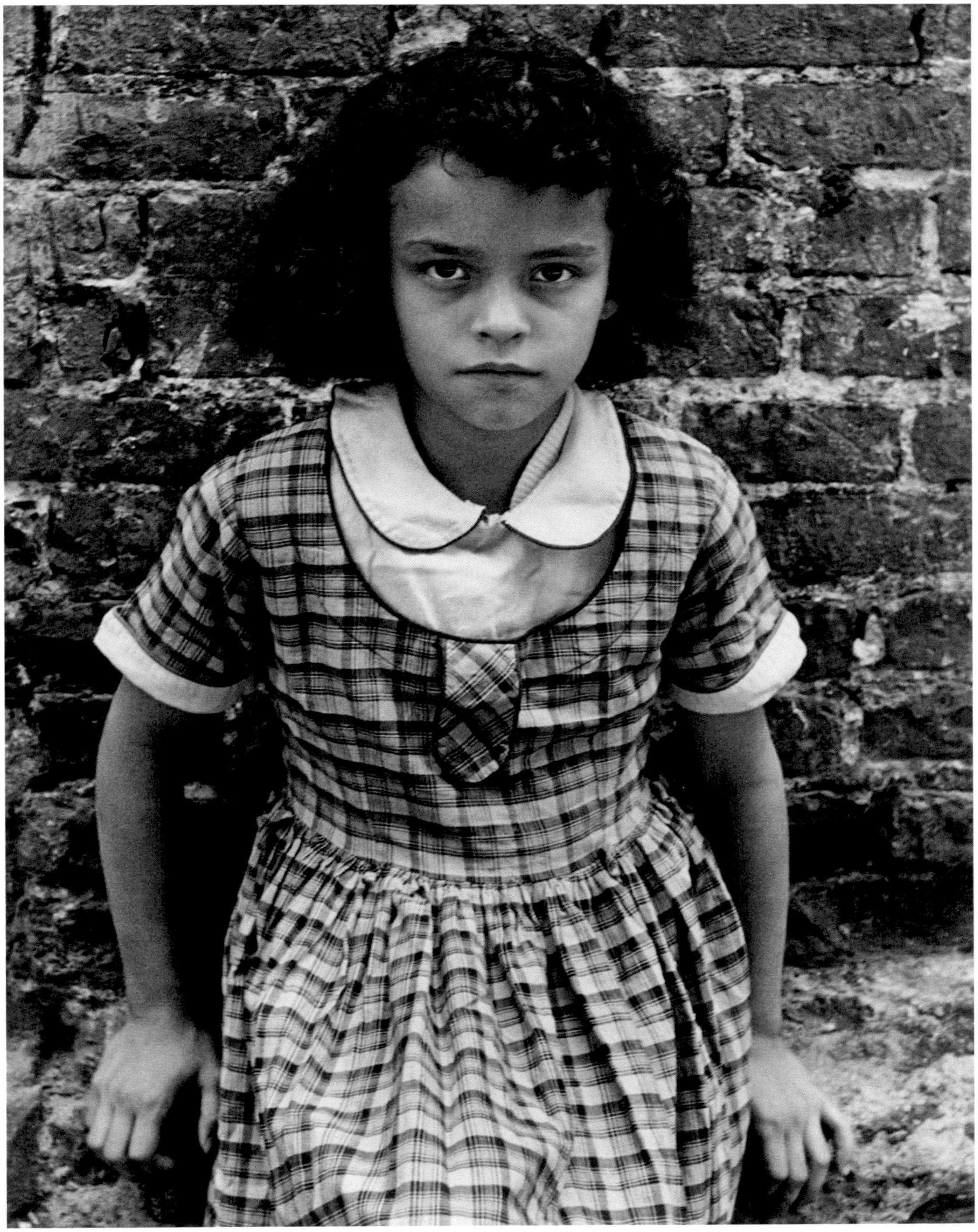

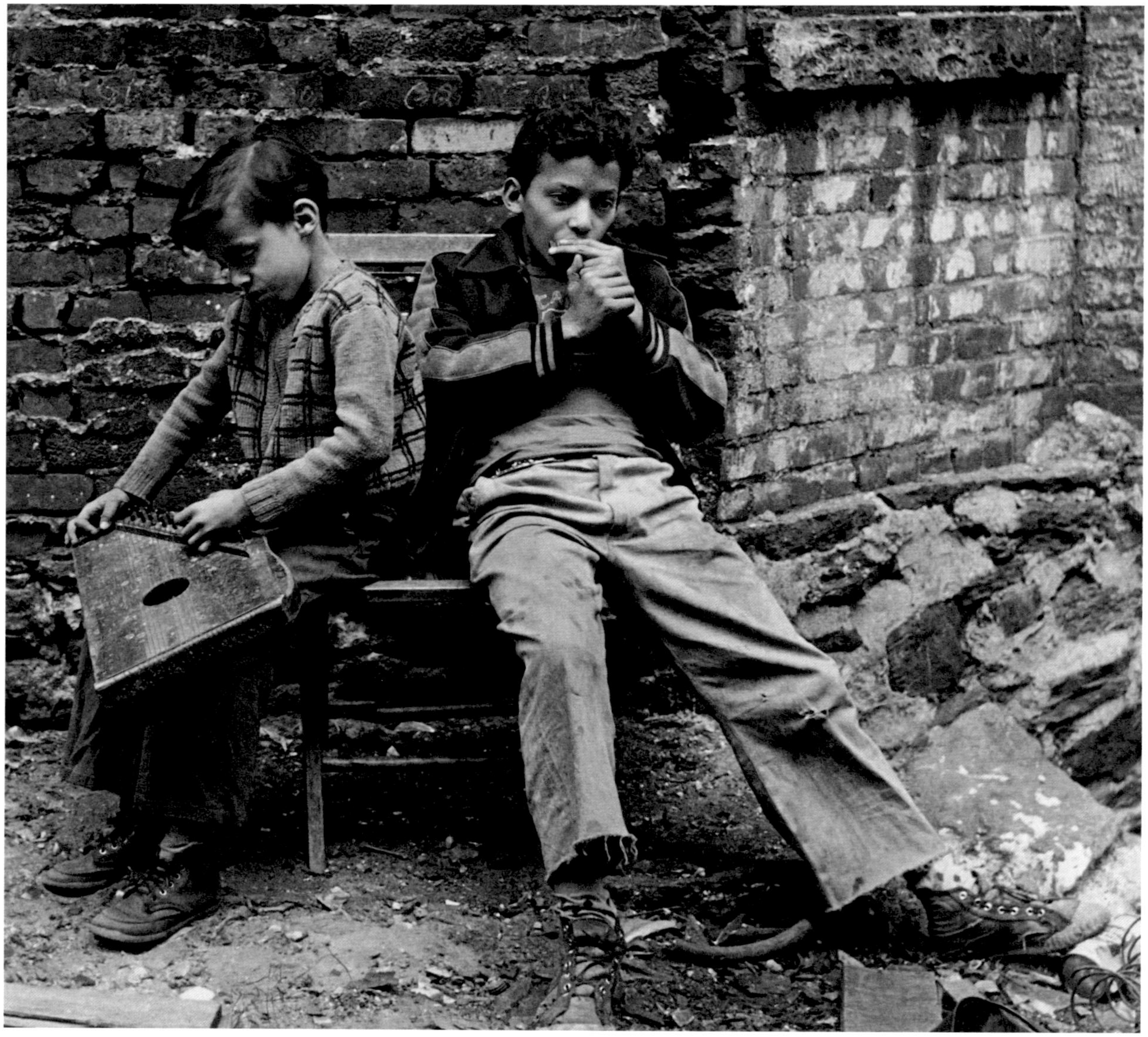

Two friends playing instruments, c. 1950

Paper fire, c. 1950

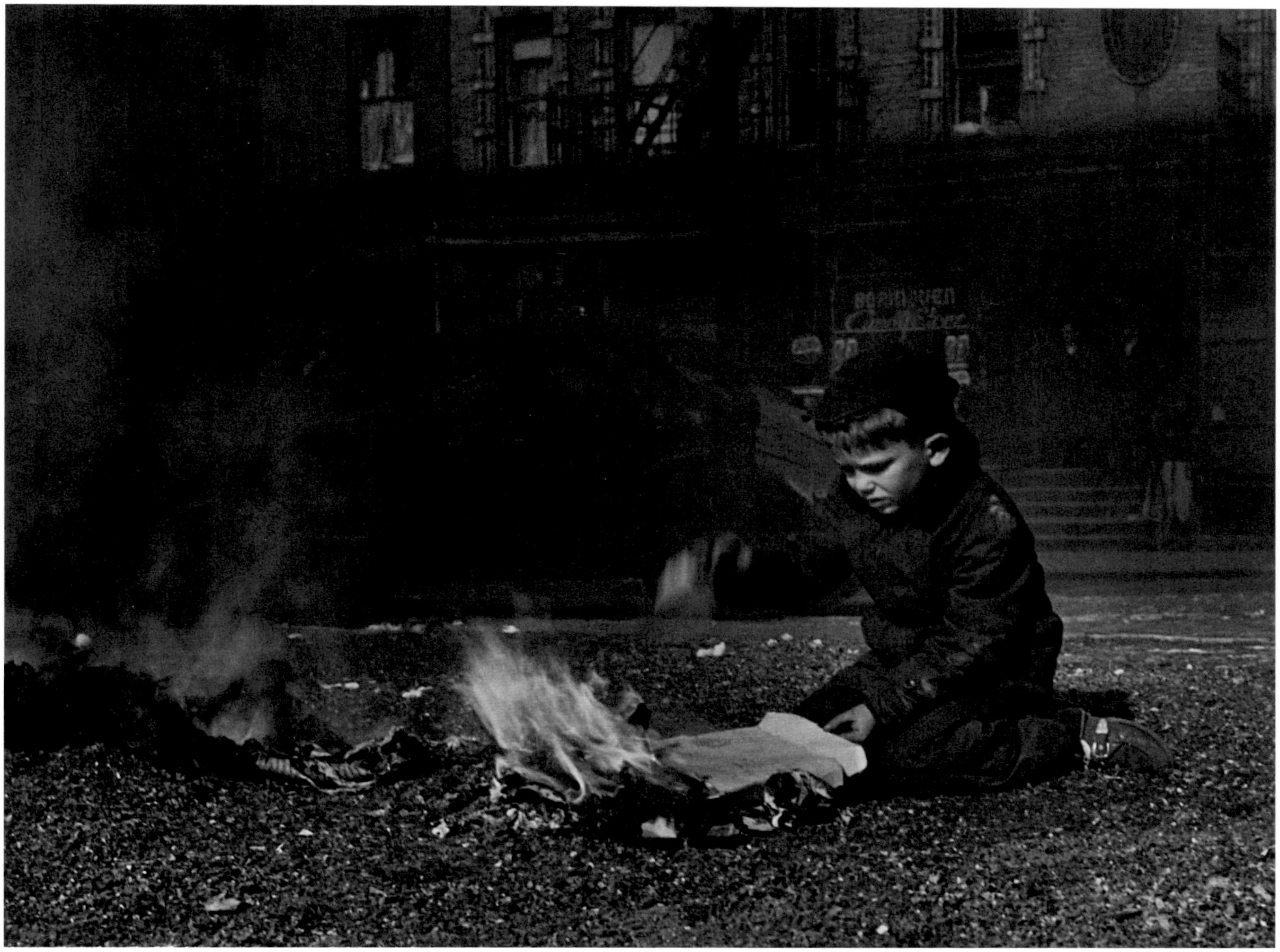

 Blind accordion player, c. 1950

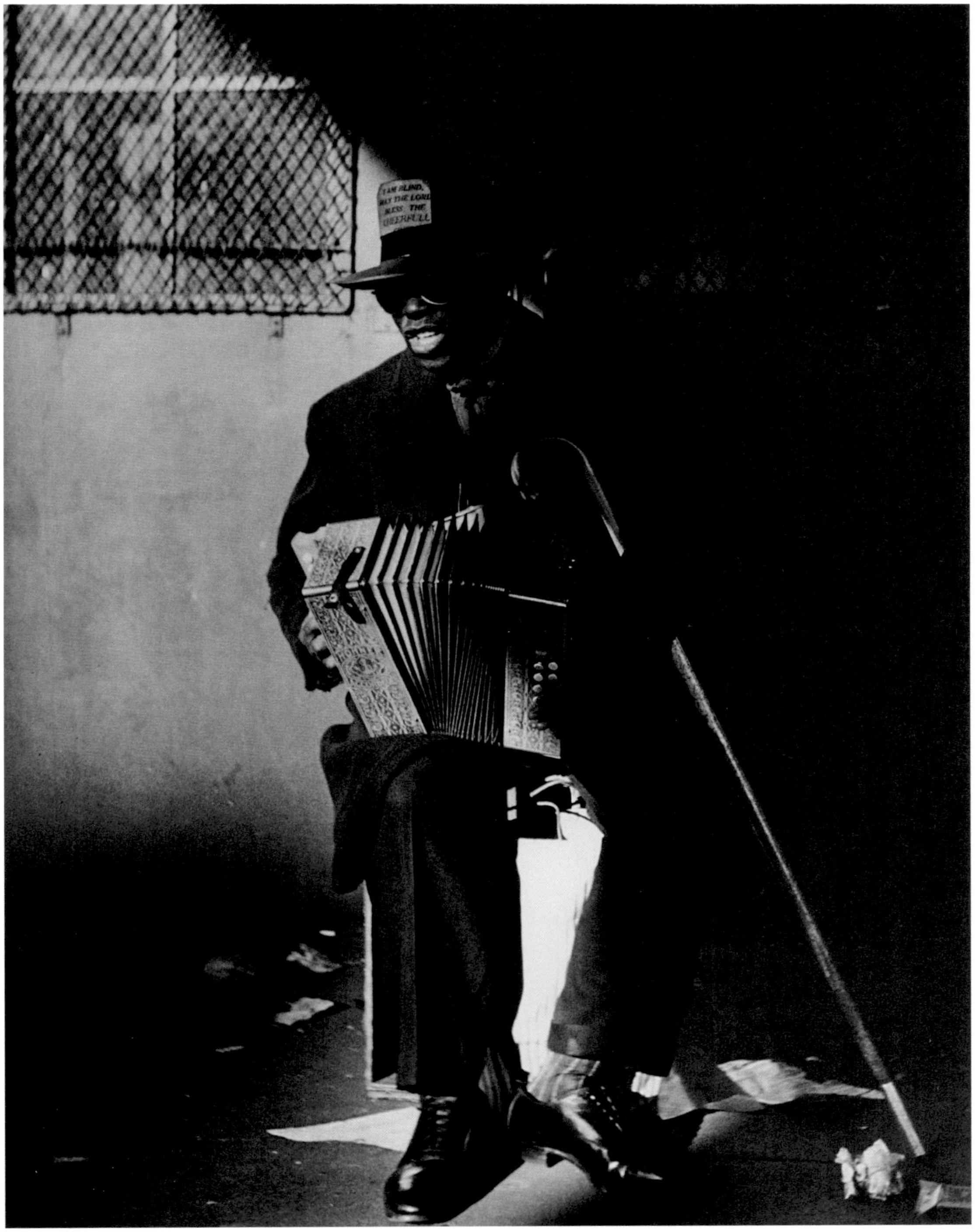
I AM BLIND,

 Portrait of a boy, c. 1950

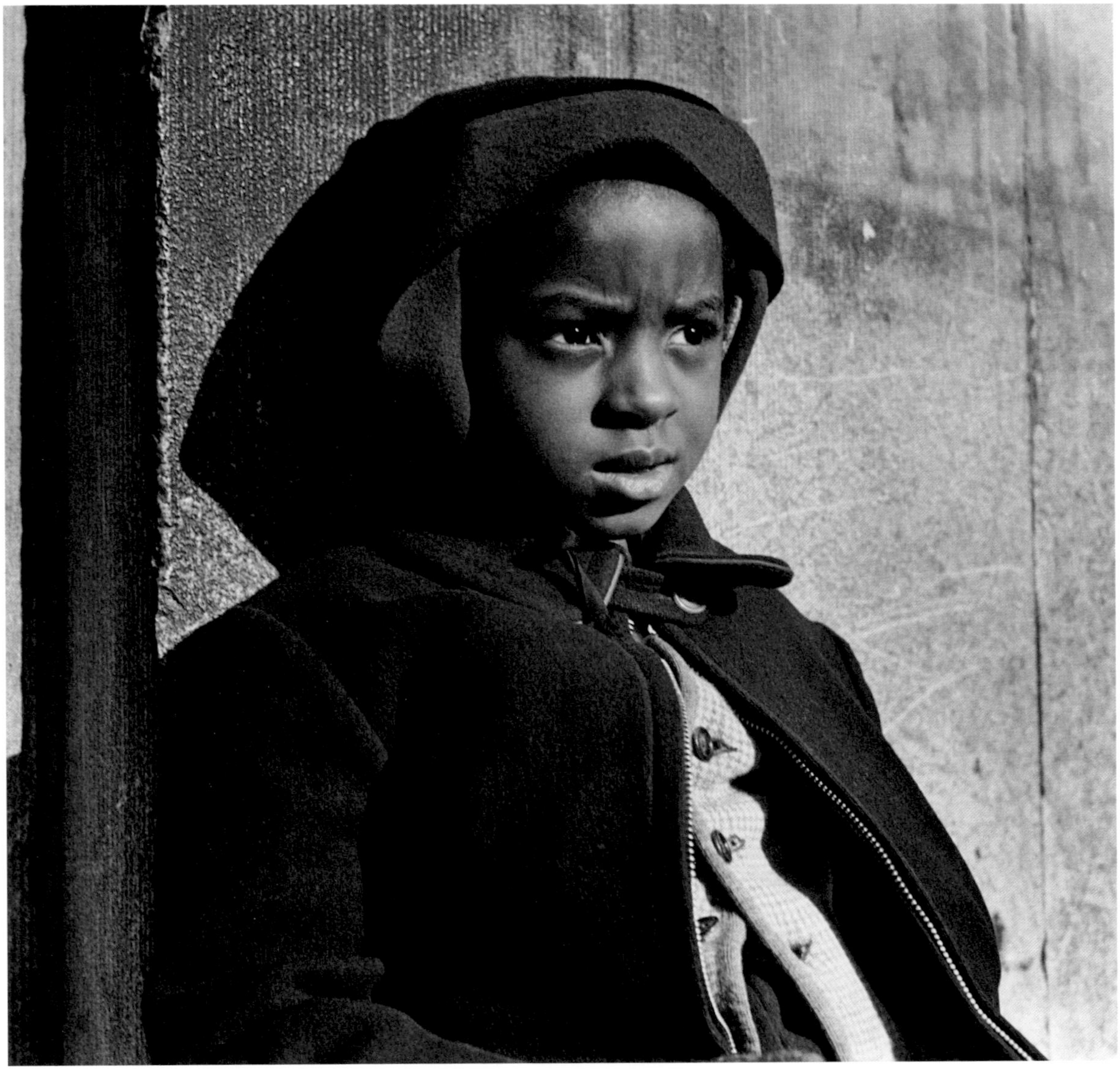

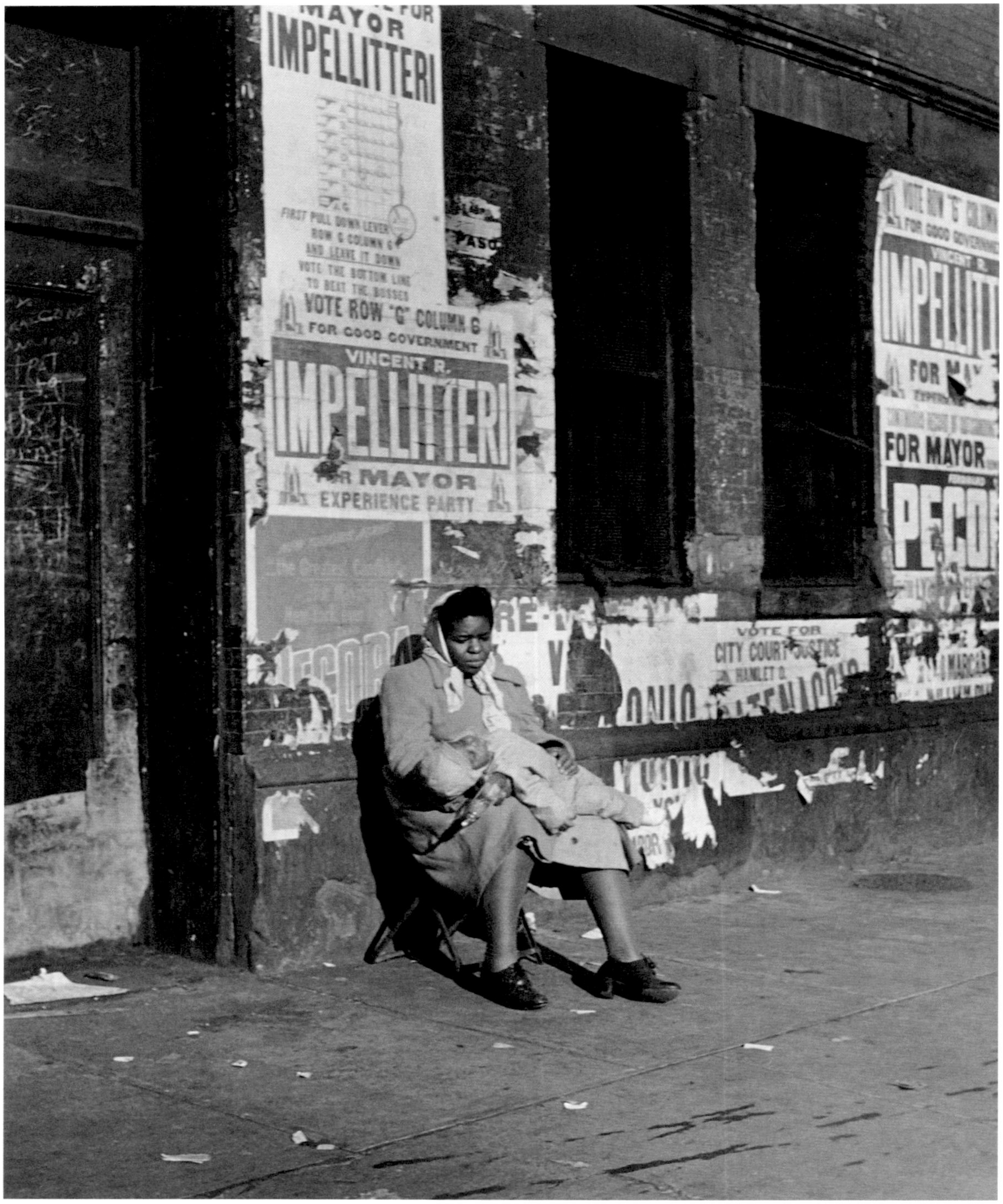
MAYOR
IMPELLITTERI
FIRST PULL DOWN LEVER
ROW G COLUMN 6
AND LEAVE IT DOWN
VOTE THE BOTTOM LINE
TO BEAT THE BOSSES
VOTE ROW "G" COLUMN 6
FOR GOOD GOVERNMENT
VINCENT R.
IMPELLITTERI
MAYOR
EXPERIENCE PARTY
VINCENT R.
FOR MAYOR
VOTE FOR
CITY COURT JUSTICE

Mother seated with child, c. 1950

132 Doorway with carriage, c. 1950

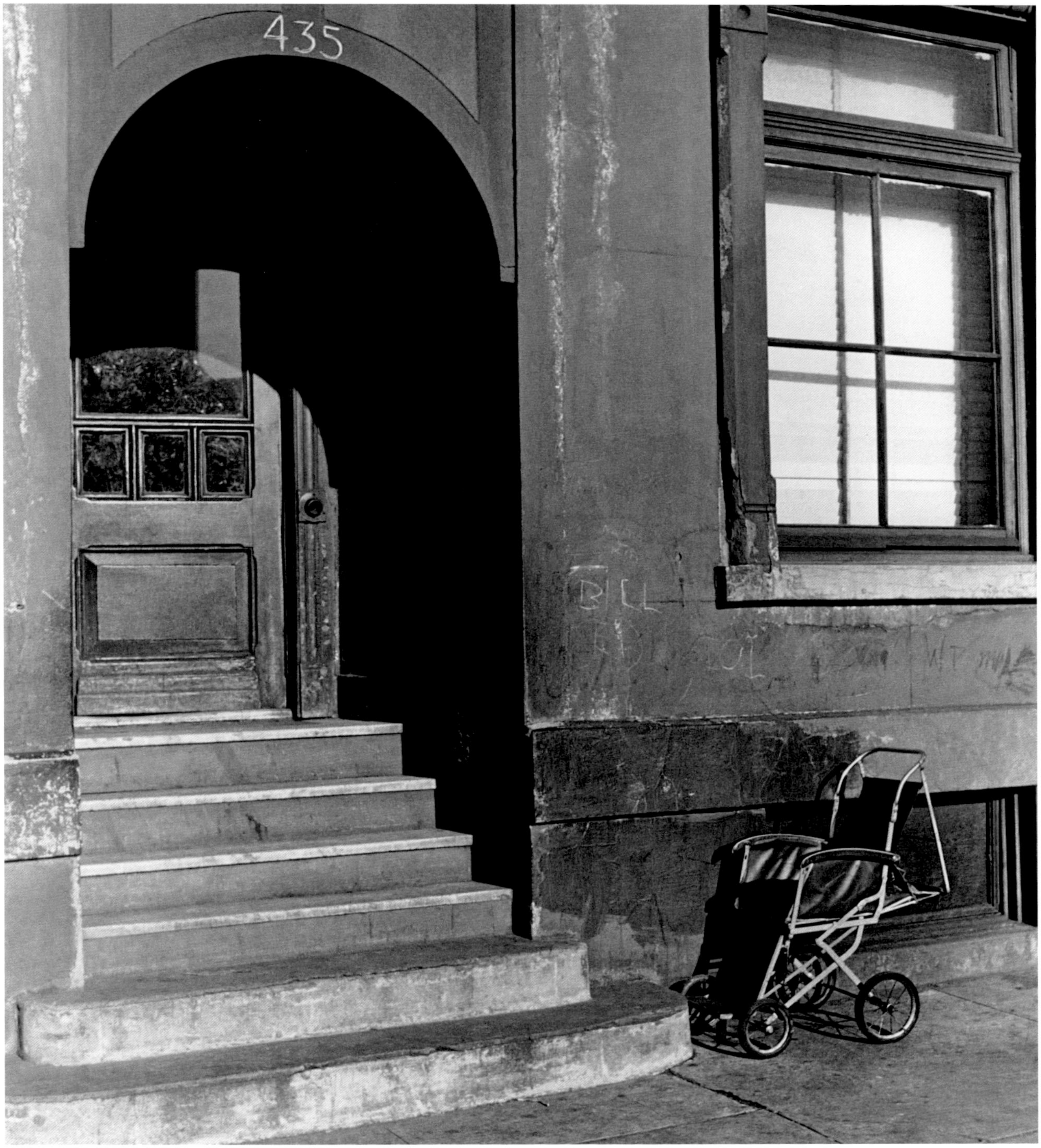
435
BILL

Condemned building, c. 1950. Note: Old tenement buildings in large sections of the community were condemned and torn down to make way for New York City public housing projects.

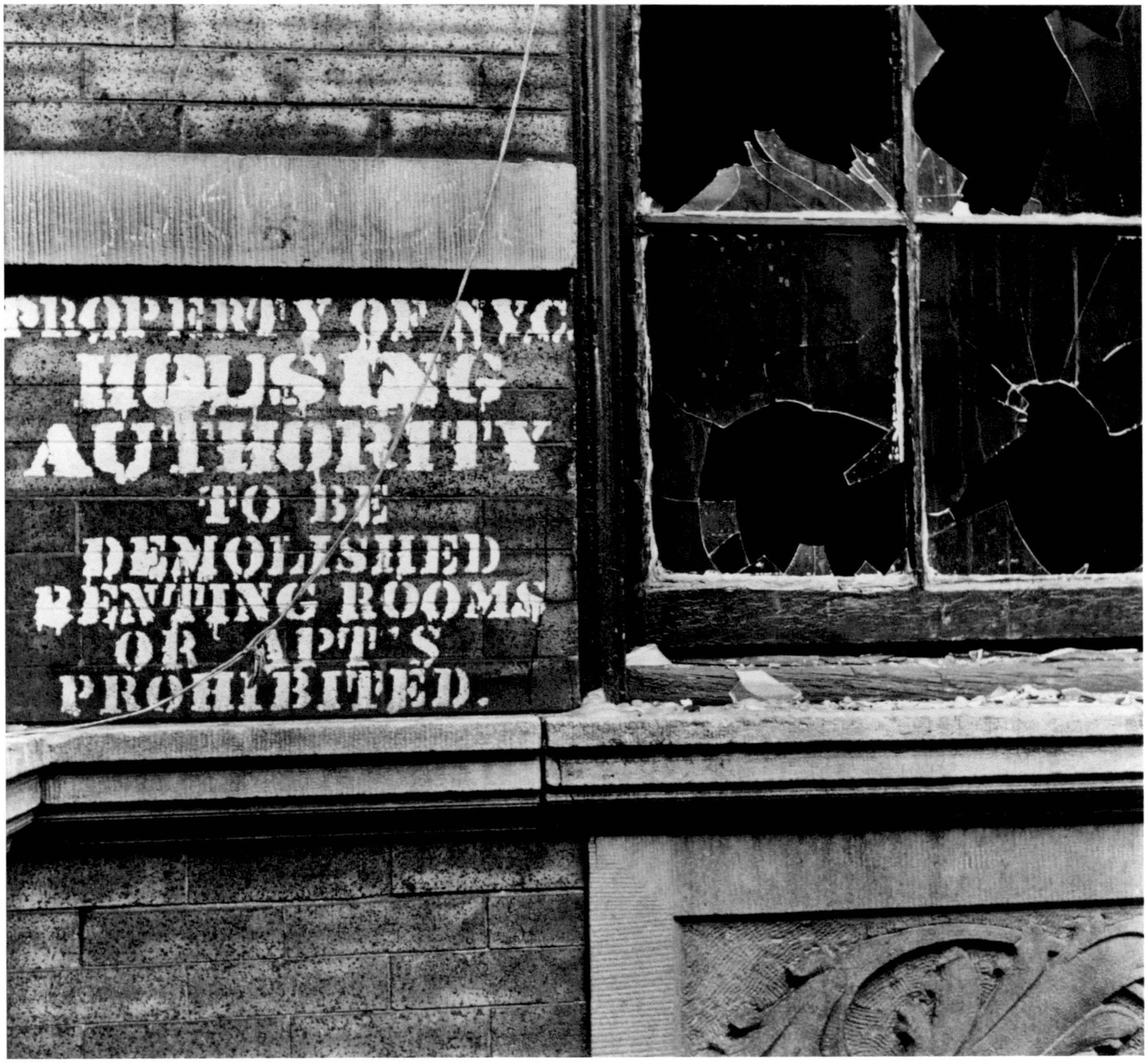
PROPERTY OF N.Y.C.
HOUSING
AUTHORITY
TO BE
DEMOLISHED
RENTING ROOMS
OR APT'S
PROHIBITED.

 Demolition site, c. 1950

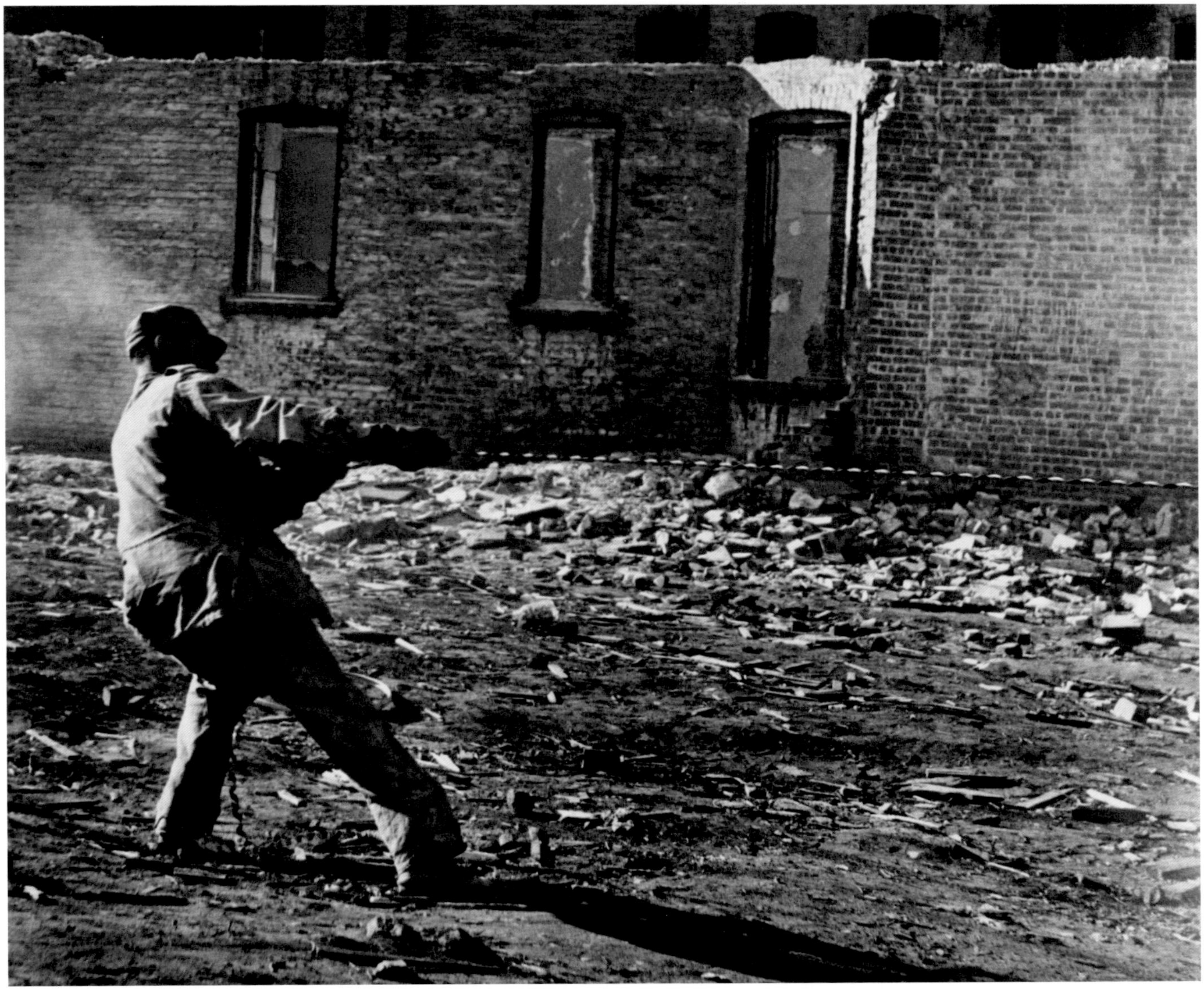

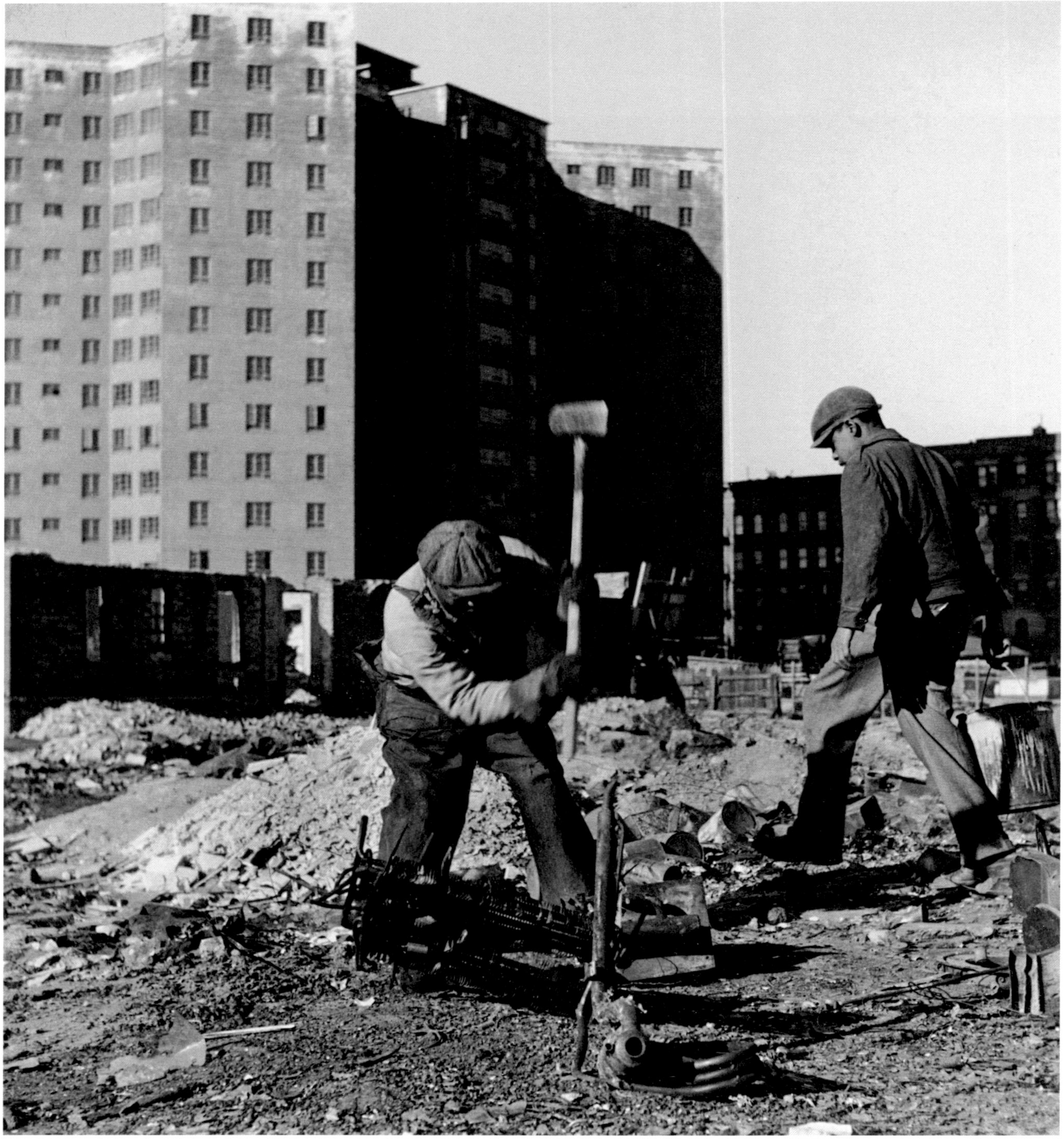

 Gathering scrap metal at site cleared for public housing, c. 1950

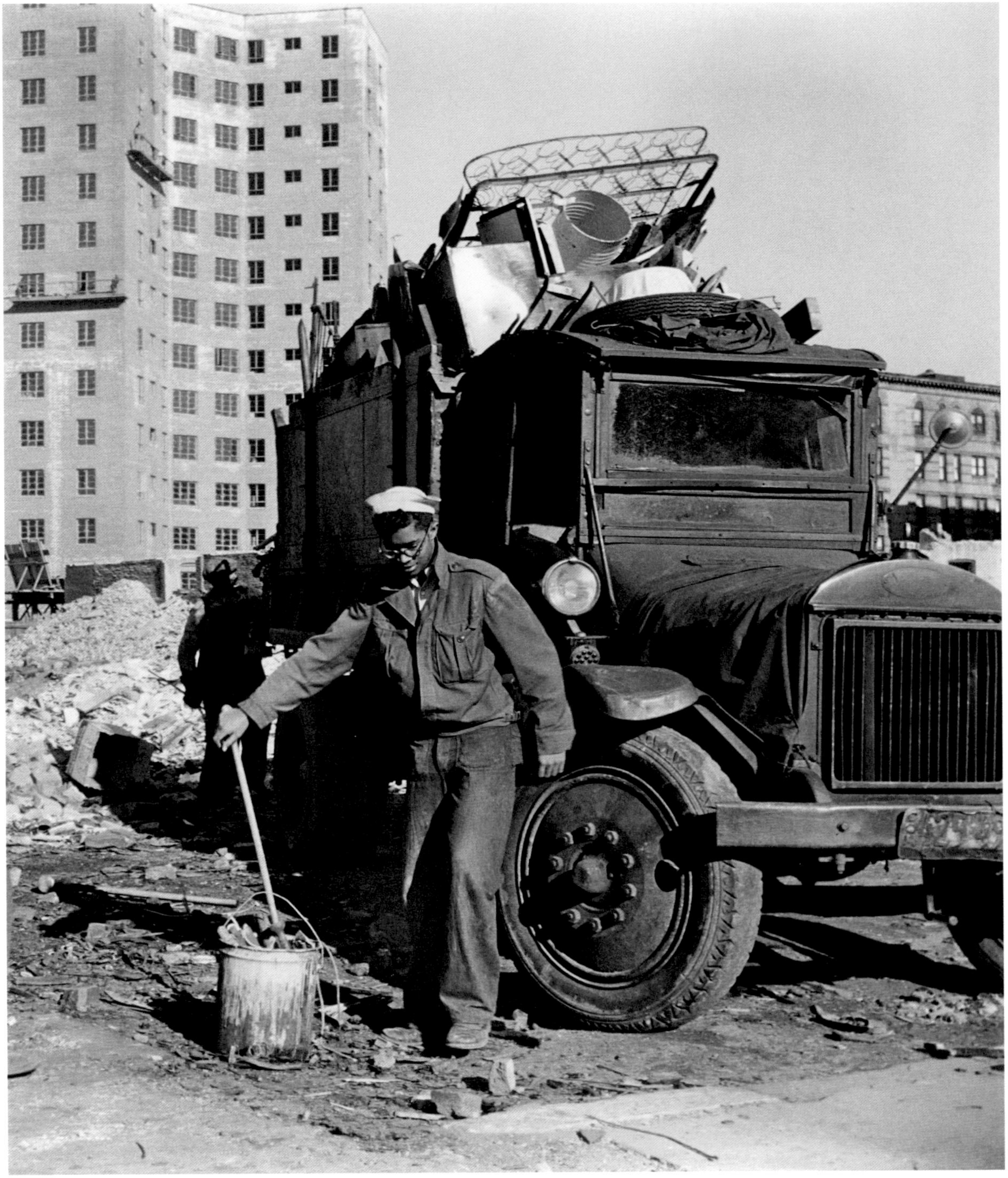

Carting away scrap metal, c. 1950

 Site cleared for public housing, c. 1950

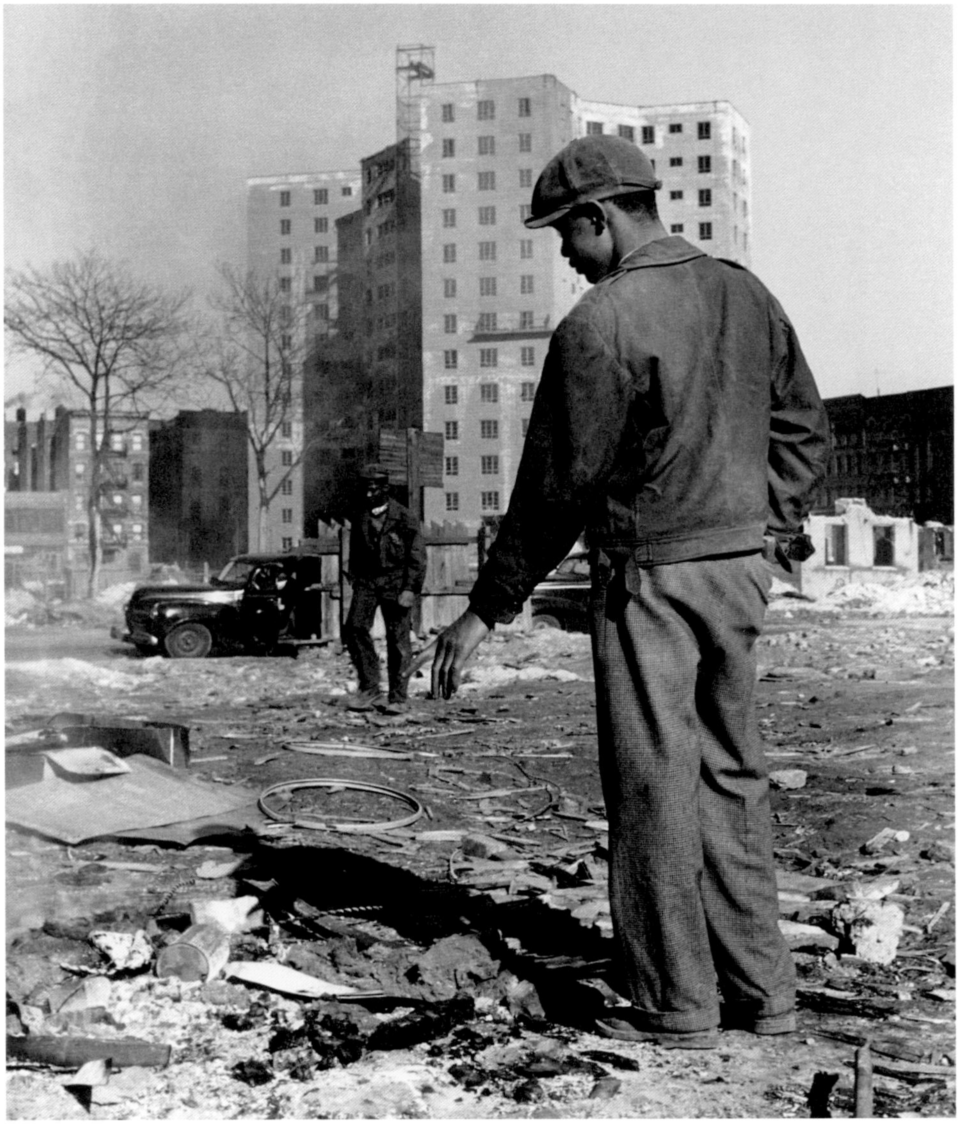

 Climbing the fence, c. 1950

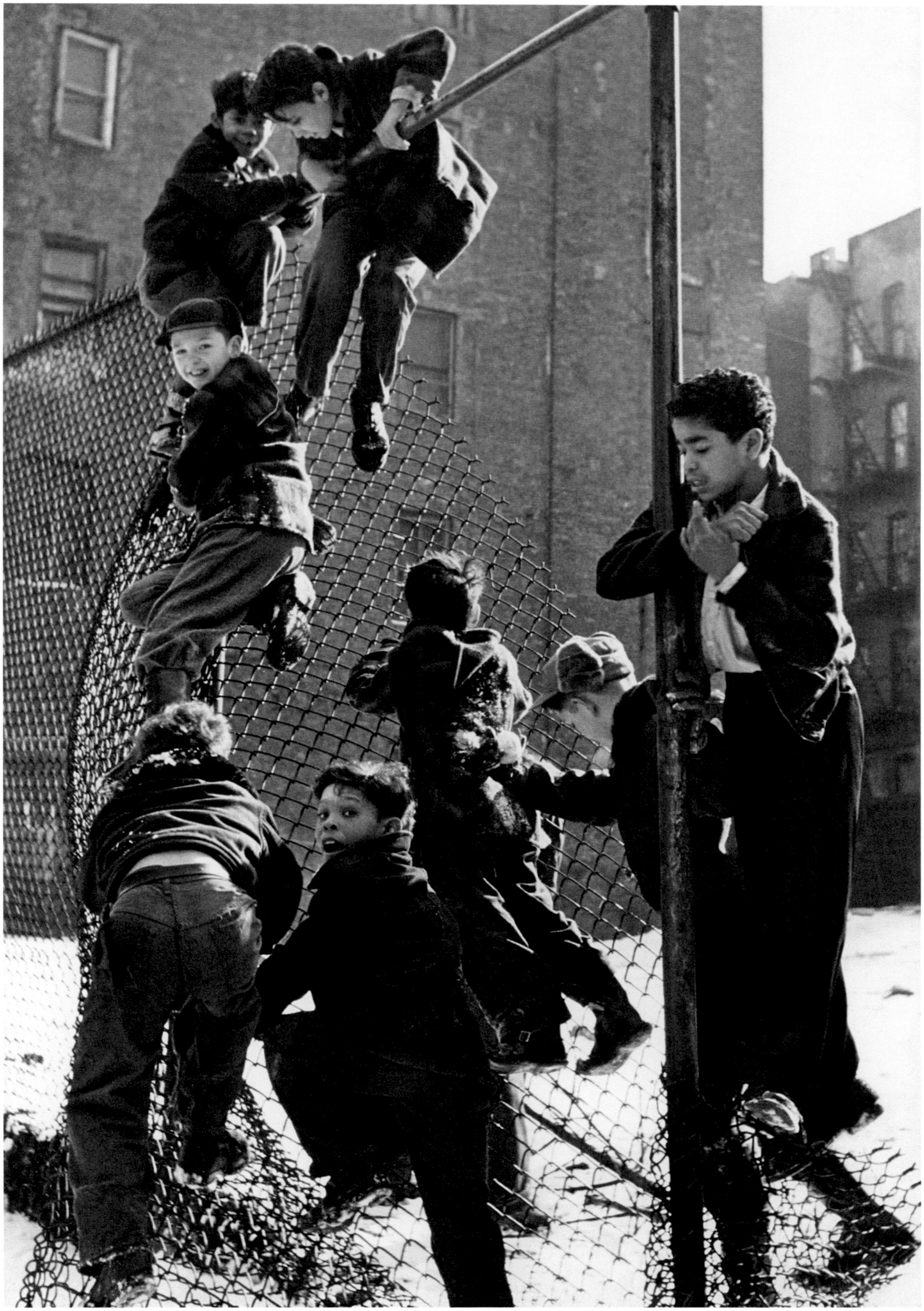

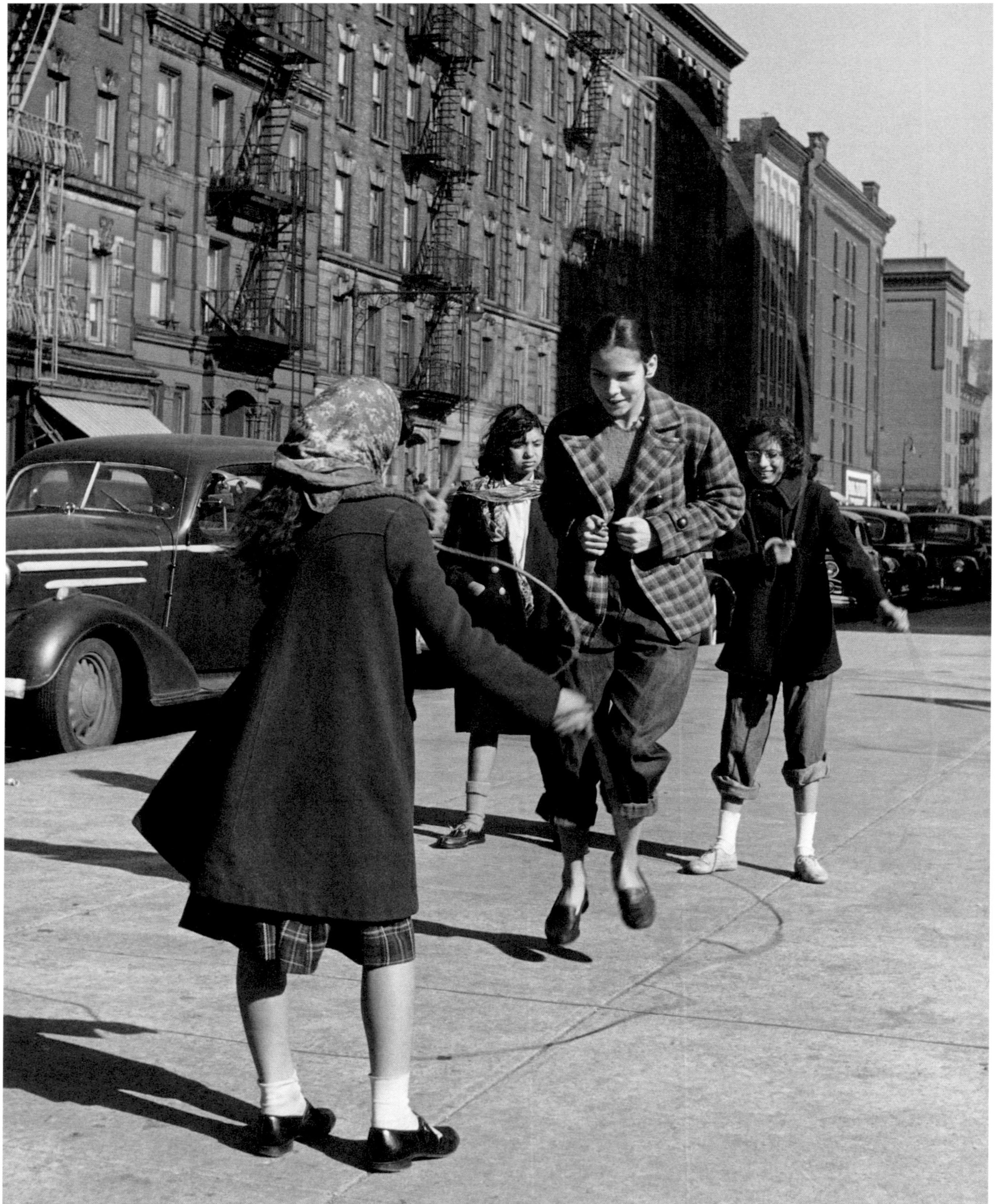

Girls playing on East 110th Street, 1952

146 Street singer and girl collecting money, c. 1950

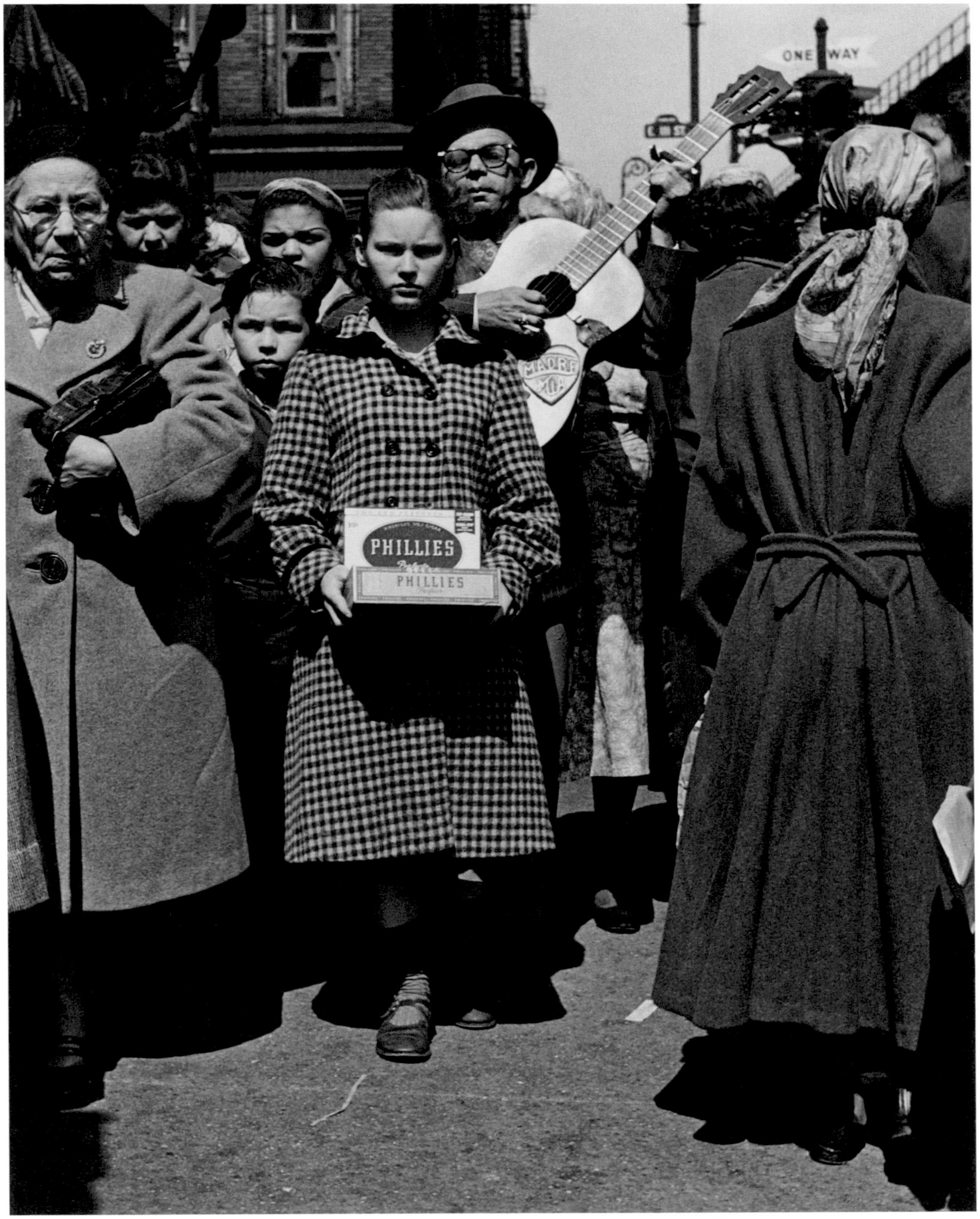
ONE WAY
PHILLIES
PHILLIES

Shopping day at La Marqueta, c. 1950

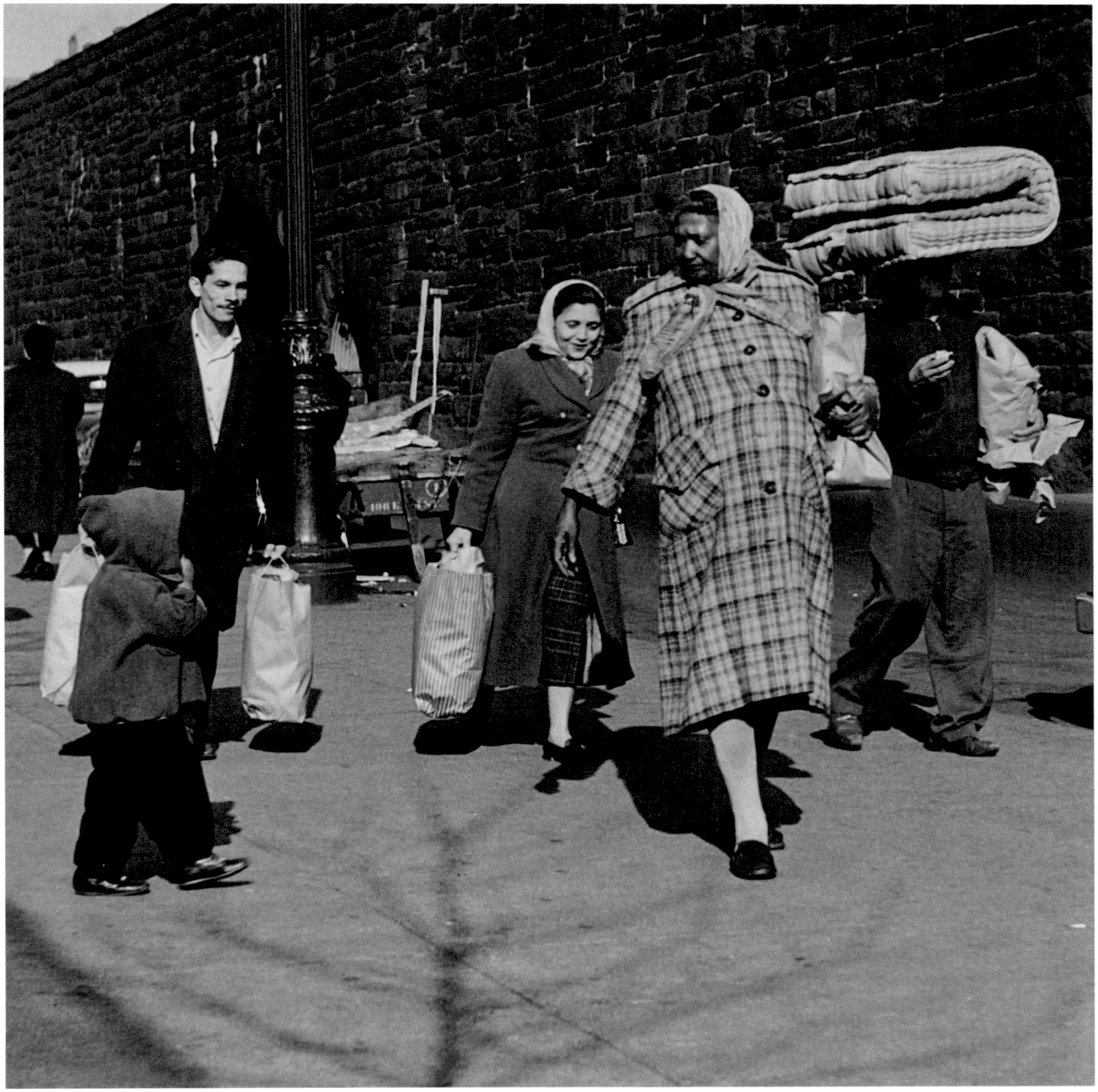

Little girl with hat, c. 1950

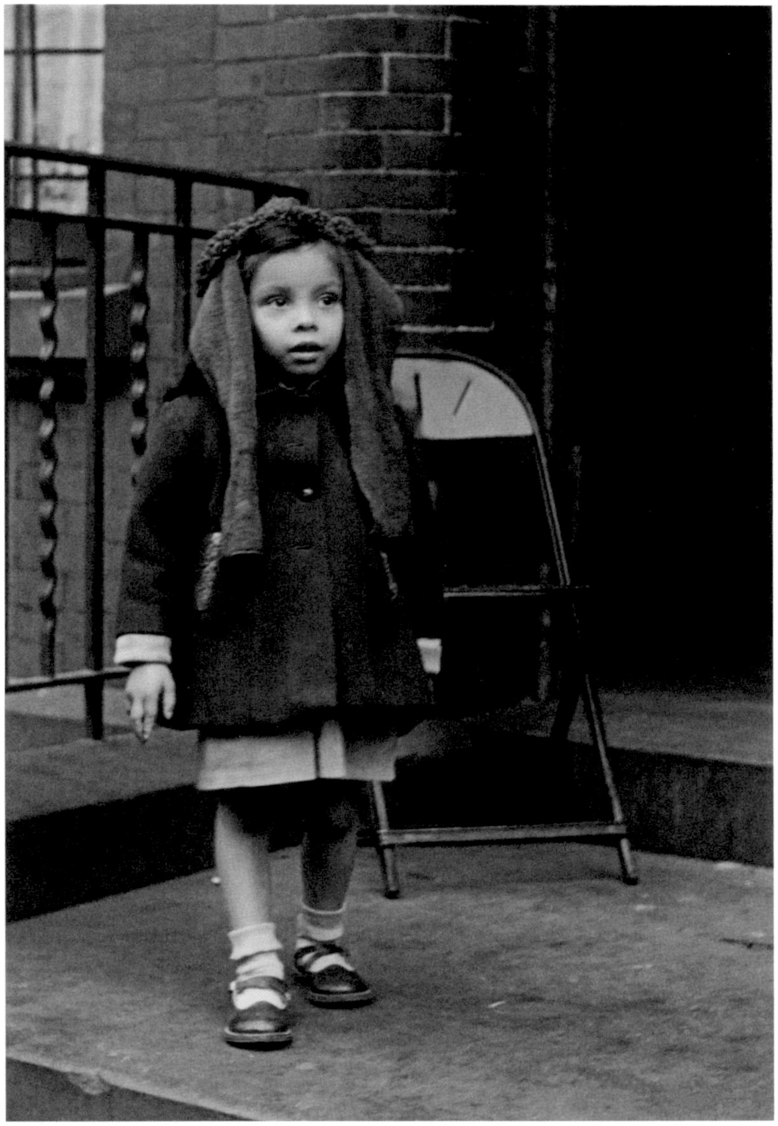

Chico florist cart, East 100th Street, winter, 1951

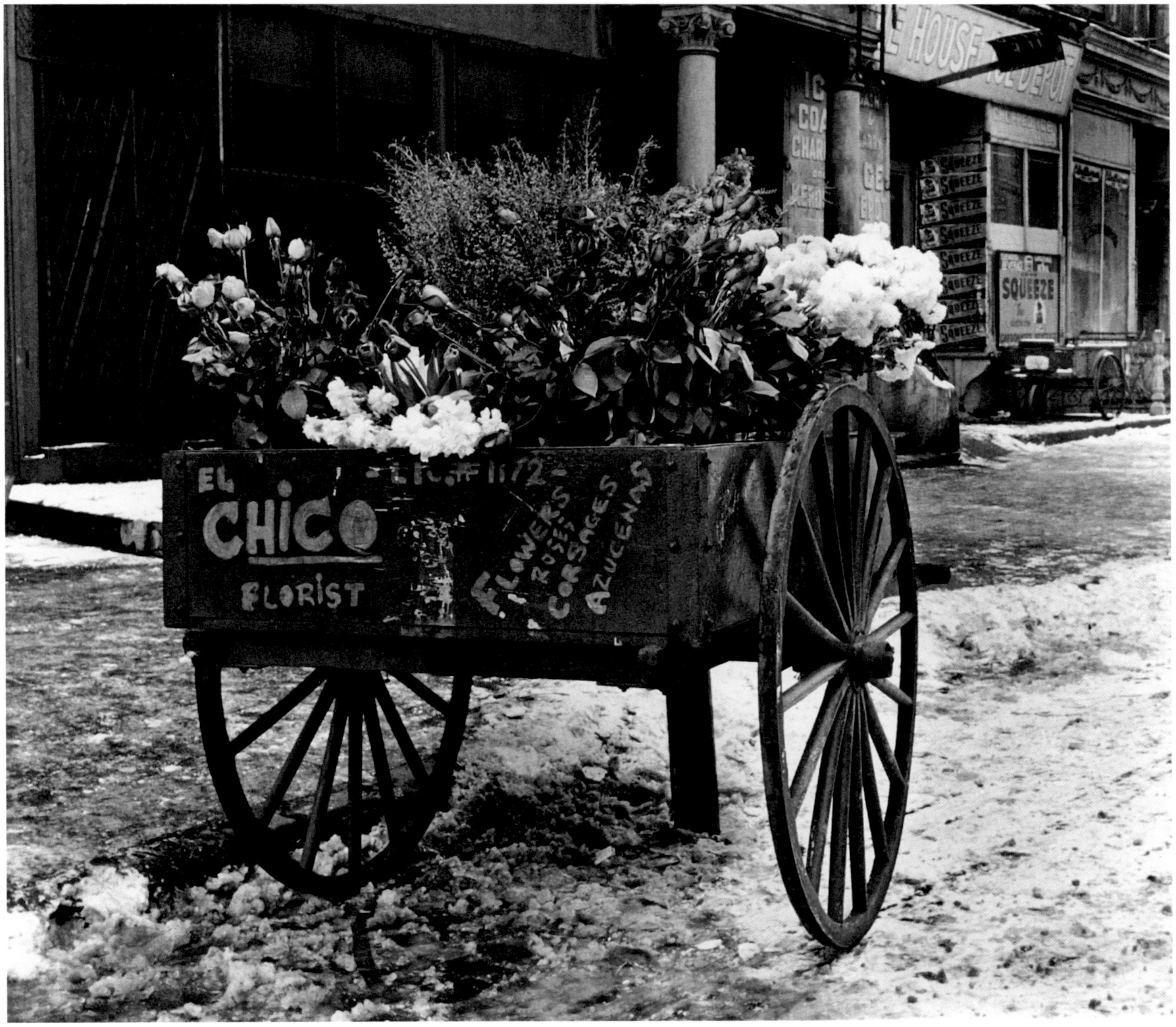
EL
CHICO
FLORIST
FLOWERS
ROSES
CORSAGES
AZUCENAS
SQUEEZE

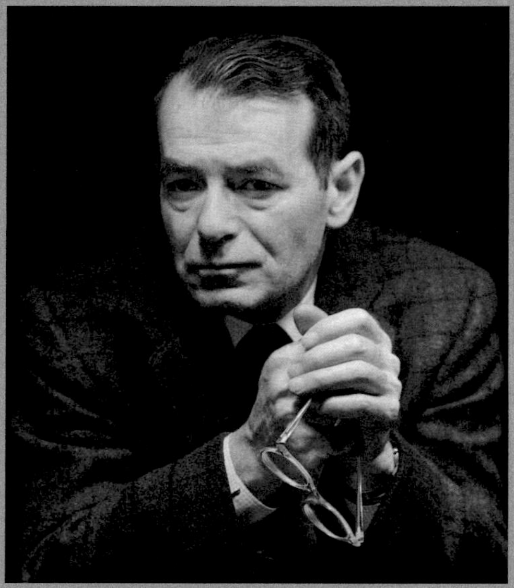

Leo Goldstein

About the Artist

Leo Goldstein was born in 1901 in Kishinev in the Bessarabian region (now Moldova) of Czarist Russia. Fleeing the pogroms, his family first settled on the Lower East Side of New York City in 1906. Leo was the fourth of 13 children and went to work at an early age to help support the large family. As a young man he studied sculpture and was a talented amateur artist, taking up photography when he joined the Photo League in the late 1940s.

He threw himself into the social documentary tradition of the League, turning his lens, as many of the League members did, to the migrant and poor communities in New York City. He was greatly influenced by the work of Paul Strand, Lewis Hine, and Berenice Abbott, among other members.

With the body of work from East Harlem, which is collected here for the first time, Leo left us an important and unique addition to the Harlem and Lower East Side studies done earlier by Photo League members. Because his family had lived in East Harlem for a time as part of an earlier generation of migrants, Leo was familiar with the streets, the tenements, and the building stoops where neighbors gathered to sit, talk, and watch their children play.

Beginning in 1949, and over several years, Leo photographed in East Harlem using a Rolleiflex twin-lens camera that he had bought secondhand. He lived in an apartment building on West 83rd Street and built a darkroom in the basement where he developed all his negatives. Leo's son Fred remembers that his father worked very hard on the printing process, printing his images over and over again to get the light and dark areas just as he wanted them.

Leo believed that developing and printing his own photographs was as much a part of his creative process as taking the picture itself. To illustrate how strongly he believed this, Leo declined an invitation to submit negatives for use in the *Family of Man* exhibition because he felt that to have someone else print an image from his negative would not truly represent his work.

Portrait of Leo Goldstein by Bernard Cole

Even after the League was targeted by the FBI as a subversive organization and forced to disband in 1951, Leo and a number of former members continued to meet at each other's homes on a round-robin basis to show and critique their work. According to Fred, some of those whom he remembers meeting this way were Walter Rosenblum, Bernard "Barney" Cole, Jack Lessinger, Ida Berman, and Sam Mahl, among others.

In addition to East Harlem, Leo photographed in Mexico and Guatemala in the 1960s. He was close to Paul Strand and kept in touch with him after the League was disbanded. Strand's influence on Leo was clear in the portraits he took of people in Mexico. Leo also took a series of photographs in the Vermont countryside during the same period. An interest in preserving a record of some of the beautiful buildings in New York City neighborhoods led him to photograph a series of buildings in Brooklyn. That latter body of work is now housed in the archives of the Museum of the City of New York.

In the late 1960s, Leo began a major project to photograph stone carvings on old buildings, mainly on the Upper West Side of Manhattan where he lived. As an amateur sculptor himself, Leo was particularly concerned about preserving these artistic expressions, which might be destroyed as part of the process of gentrification in the city. He was working toward the publication of a book of these images when he became ill and died.

Following Leo's death in 1972, none of his negatives could be found. They may have been discarded when his darkroom was dismantled. This illustrates how little was known about the value of the work at that time.

A small number of Leo's images have appeared in exhibits and publications of Photo League work, beginning with the seminal exhibit *This Is the Photo League* (1948–1949) and later in the book, *This Was the Photo League*, published by the Stephen Daiter Gallery and John

Cleary Gallery in 2001. His work was included in "The Photo League, 1936–1951," an exhibition organized by Howard Greenberg at the Photofind Gallery in Woodstock, New York in 1985. One of Leo's images was also included in the 2011–12 exhibit at the Jewish Museum entitled "The Radical Camera: New York's Photo League, 1936–1951." The vast majority of his photographs have never been shown or reproduced.

Until 2016, when the prints were catalogued, this body of work remained mostly untouched and unseen. The 70 vintage prints reproduced here are part of a larger collection of East Harlem photographs consisting of over 250 silver gelatin vintage prints made by the artist.

Because there are no negatives remaining, it was of particular importance to preserve the photographs in book form in order to make them available to a wider audience.

— NAOMI GOLDSTEIN

Acknowledgments

Leo Goldstein's photographs were stored in cardboard boxes, beginning in the late 1940s, until his death in 1972. With few exceptions, they remained hidden away until 1996, when his wife, Bess Goldstein, died and his son, Fred Goldstein, and I inherited them. In the year 2000, I began to go through the boxes, sort the photographs into categories, and put them into archival sleeves. Particularly because there were no negatives remaining, we had always hoped to preserve Leo's work by publishing a book.

A number of individuals played a part in making this monograph possible. However, Régina Monfort is the person who was key to finally getting it done. We met by chance at a gathering of the American Photography Archives Group (APAG) in 2014. An accomplished photographer and a visual book editor experienced with archives, she immediately recognized the significance of the photographs my father-in-law had taken in East Harlem and asked to see more. Thus began our collaboration on the book presented here.

Régina helped me organize and catalog, for the first time, the original vintage prints. She edited and sequenced the images, secured an anonymous donation of digital captures of the prints, oversaw the postproduction work on the digital files, and found the publisher. It was really her generous dedication to the project that made it possible for Leo Goldstein's East Harlem photographs to finally see the light of day.

We are grateful to Pedro Juan Hernández, Senior Archivist at the Center for Puerto Rican Studies at Hunter College (CUNY) with whom we shared the images and who helped us reach out to a number of scholars in the field. Among them was Dr. Virginia Sánchez Korrol, a historian and professor emerita in the Department of Puerto Rican and Latino Studies at Brooklyn College, CUNY. We thank her for encouraging us to keep going and for introducing us to Juan González. We also thank Dr. Andrés Torres, Distinguished Lecturer at Lehman College, for his interest in the work.

We thank Juan González for sharing his childhood memories of living in East Harlem and for contributing his expertise and moving commentary on the large postwar migration of Puerto Ricans to this neighborhood.

We thank A. D. Coleman for contributing his extensive knowledge of photography and Photo League history to this book and for lending his authoritative voice to the introduction.

Howard Greenberg was there at the beginning, when he included Leo's work in an exhibition about the Photo League that he curated in 1985. Years later, when Régina and I showed Howard the East Harlem photographs as a body of work, he encouraged us to apply to the Phillip and Edith Leonian Foundation for funding.

We thank Mary Engel, APAG founder, for creating an organization dedicated to the preservation of photographic archives and for always being available to give helpful advice; thanks also to Michael Kamber, founder and director of the Bronx Documentary Center, for his appreciation of the work and kind support; and to Kathleen Haskins and Hiram Maristany, who helped to identify some of the locations of the photographs. Maristany, a lifelong resident of East Harlem and photographer, has been documenting life in El Barrio through photographs since the 1960s.

Régina Monfort would like to extend her special thanks to Patrice Pascual and Julia Van Haaften for believing in this book early on; Bob Shamis for his friendly advice; Julia Wang and Nicola Dracoulis for their assistance; Colin Strohm for his digital expertise; Melanie Einzig and Geneviève Hafner for their friendship, keen eyes, and love of photography; and to Emily Schiffer for bringing her sensibility and talent to the retouching of the images.

We deeply appreciate the commitment of Daniel Power and Craig Cohen from powerHouse Books to publish this monograph even before they had seen the full selection of East Harlem photographs. They brought together a highly dedicated and talented team including managing editor Will Luckman, and graphic designer Francesca Richer, who contributed the thoughtful and elegant design of the book. They were a pleasure to work with.

Thanks to the Phillip and Edith Leonian Foundation, which provided a grant that funded, in part, the publication of this book. In addition, we received crucial and generous support from Jim and Melissa O'Shaughnessy, as well as my sister, Ellen Catalinotto, who also provided valuable feedback on the texts and design.

Leo's son and my partner, Fred Goldstein, encouraged me to publish this work and lent support at every phase of the process, even when it seemed to be an impossible task. He shared his memories of his father's photographic work and remembered the circle of Photo League friends who met at his home.

Leo's granddaughters, Carla and Lila Goldstein, gave us essential feedback on the essays as well as design ideas and moral support. Their enthusiasm helped us to keep going. We also thank Leo's nephew, Phil Galdston, for providing documentation of the Goldstein family history.

It is now 70 years since Leo began to take the photographs included in this book. We are grateful to everyone who played a part in helping to preserve and disseminate these images of the East Harlem community from so long ago.

— NAOMI GOLDSTEIN

EAST HARLEM: The Postwar Years

Published in the United States by powerHouse Books,
a division of powerHouse Cultural Entertainment, Inc.
32 Adams Street, Brooklyn, NY 11201-1021
e-mail: info@powerHouseBooks.com
website: www.powerHouseBooks.com

First edition, 2019

Library of Congress Control Number: 2019941652

ISBN 978-1-57687-930-6

Editing and sequencing of photographs by Régina Monfort
Book design by Francesca Richer
Printed by EBS Editoriale Bortolazzi, Verona

10 9 8 7 6 5 4 3 2 1

Printed and bound in Italy

The publication of this book was made possible, in part, by a grant from the Phillip and Edith Leonian Foundation.